IMAGES
of America

SAN FRANCISCO'S NOB HILL

ON THE COVER: In this World War II–era image, a parade makes its way along California Street, past the Fairmont Hotel, the Pacific-Union Club, and Huntington Park.

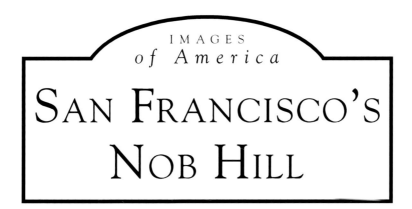

IMAGES
of America

SAN FRANCISCO'S
NOB HILL

Katherine Powell Cohen

ARCADIA
PUBLISHING

Published by Arcadia Publishing
Charleston, South Carolina

Printed in the United States of America

Library of Congress Control Number: 2010926869

For all general information, please contact Arcadia Publishing:
Telephone 843-853-2070
Fax 843-853-0044
E-mail sales@arcadiapublishing.com
For customer service and orders:
Toll-Free 1-888-313-2665

Visit us on the Internet at www.arcadiapublishing.com

For Phil E., Tom, and Everett P.—
my favorite gentlemen to lunch with on Nob Hill

CONTENTS

ACKNOWLEDGMENTS

To Grace Cathedral archivist Michael Lampen, for providing me with his time and efforts and materials, as well as space to work, I am very grateful. All photographs not otherwise credited were provided by Grace Cathedral Archives. My gratitude goes also to Ron Henggeler, historian, photographer, longtime fixture at the Huntington Hotel's Big Four restaurant, gentleman, and rare soul. Phil Elissetche, historian and keeper of the grounds at Huntington Park, is a kind friend, and I thank him. Thomas Wolfe, concierge extraordinaire at the Fairmont, gracefully facilitated my research. The Fairmont's Samara Diapoulos and David Rich kindly took the time to provide essential photographs. Thanks also to Connie Perez of Intercontinental Hotels for her assistance in acquiring photographs of the Mark Hopkins. Roger Tyler of Grace Cathedral made a very special contribution to my research. I'm also grateful to The Nob Hill Association, and especially Stephen Patton, David Lefkowitz, and Fran Hildebrand, without whose support this book would not have been possible. To Isabelle Fritz Cope and Serena Fritz-Cope, I'm grateful for their generosity of time, graciousness, and senses of humor. I deeply appreciate the patience and support of my daughter, Meredyth "Miriam" Powell Cohen, my husband, Jeff Cohen, and my parents, the Rev. Dr. Everett Powell and Gloria Powell. Special thanks go to the people at the Apple Store Genius Bar and the amazingly helpful people at DriveSavers. To my editor, John Poultney, I owe enormous gratitude. His combination of patience, serenity, and efficiency is rare.

INTRODUCTION

The first houses reached the windy upper slopes of Nob Hill in 1853, thirty million years after runoff from a faraway island met with the continent to form a land mass that includes today's Nob Hill, Russian Hill, Telegraph Hill, Alcatraz, and Yerba Buena Island. Nob Hill consists of sandstone and shale. Coastanoan natives have lived in the area for at least 6,000 years, but it is probable that the first Ohlones, a tribe established in what is now San Francisco, came to the north end of the peninsula in the sixth century C.E. Michael Lampen's writing tells that these people found a hill that was sandy on its western slope, where lupine, coastal sage, coyote brush, and wild strawberry were hearty plants that managed to thrive. On the leeward northern and eastern slopes, buckeye grew among the coastal live oak, along with currants and ferns. The original inhabitants of the hill included coyotes, tule elk, deer, mountain lions, and grizzly bears. Overhead, eagles, hawks, ravens, crows, scrub jays, mourning doves, and sparrows were plentiful.

The day in 1848 when the merchant Sam Brannan rode into town and showed off a bag of gold, crying, "Gold! From the American River!," the village of 1,000 people changed drastically. During the Gold Rush, thousands of ships arrived in San Francisco, bringing many more thousands of forty-niners seeking riches in the Sierra foothills. In the first year, 100,000 people arrived. A few did strike it rich; there were others who already had financial power and came to San Francisco to increase their profits. Still others were drawn to what would be called "The Paris of the West" for the availability of work, for adventure, for an opportunity to start something new.

In 1869, six years after the first houses were built on the hill, Second Street was created south of Market Street, or the Slot, and the wealthy migrated from the Rincon Hill area to Nob Hill, then known as the Clay Street Hill. The inauguration of the Clay Street Cable Car line, the first working cable car line in the United States, in 1873, facilitated the development of grand residences atop the hill. The 1870s saw the addition of palaces built with the fortunes of railroad and mining magnates, and Clay Street Hill eventually became known as Nob Hill, probably after the term *nabobs*, connoting people of wealth and prominence.

Nob Hill still knows its nabobs, as well as the more discreet wealthy. It is also home to artists, musicians, and scholars. People from all walks of life are to be seen on the hill: an eccentric woman dressed all in white but for fire-engine red lipstick and bright pink sneakers; real estate agents dressed with attention to precision; the occasional woman in a clerical collar; the Dalai Lama himself, in his saffron robes; a smartly dressed visitor; a casually dressed tourist; a man wearing the crisp uniform of a doorman at the Huntington Hotel; an art student wearing a creative ensemble; ladies who lunch, sporting impeccable suits and the latest fashions in footwear and handbags; a group of elderly Chinese women practicing tai chi in casual elegance. Nob Hill is, like most neighborhoods in San Francisco, eclectic.

On one of those crisp, clear, still October mornings on Nob Hill, I was walking east on California Street, about to cross Taylor Street, when I noticed a man at the corner who looked to be a bit disoriented. He was at the foot of the steps of Grace Cathedral, and I was about to allow him the freedom to be a bit a bit disoriented on a morning in San Francisco, when I noticed that he was using the white cane of someone with limited eyesight. I caught his arm just before his head would have made painful contact with a parking sign. I asked if he could use a hand, and the man afforded me the honor. He pointed out that a large vehicle was parked partially blocking the crosswalk, which had caused his confusion. We chatted as we strolled arm in arm along the south side of Huntington Park, and I discovered that my companion hailed from the same part of Russia as some of my husband's ancestors. I slowed our pace outside the Pacific-Union Club and inquired, "Is this your destination?" He replied that, no, he was not a member. Realizing that the man was no longer disoriented, I prepared to be on my way but found that I was enjoying his company too much to leave him. I asked, "May I walk with you to the corner?" "I was hoping you'd walk with me around the park," he replied. I joked, "Do you often pretend not to be able to find the crosswalk?" We shared a laugh, and it was time for me to cross Mason Street to meet a friend at the Fairmont. The man (we'll call him Elijah) continued on his way, around Huntington Park and back down to his home on the western side of Nob Hill. I've caught sight of him since, walking along California Street, as he did that morning. Really, Nob Hill is full of pleasant people and delightful surprises.

Of course, there is unpleasantness, too. There have recently been unfortunate incidents involving canines and irresponsible humans, for example, and conflicts of interest among neighbors, though nothing comparable to the bullying Nicholas Yung received from Charles Crocker in the mid-1870s.

Through it all, Nob Hill remains a windy hill, a center of wealth and pageantry, and a place of spiritual pilgrimage. At the summit, in the stretch of sky visible between the towering apartment building to the east and the roofs of charming Victorian homes to the west, there is sometimes a hawk, hovering high, high above, as if nothing much has happened in the past 1,500 years.

One

AMBITION

Before Nob Hill, Rincon Hill was San Francisco's residential enclave of wealth and power, but with the development of the cable car, the steeper Nob Hill became accessible. With its stunning views, the Clay Street Hill, as it was then known, became the most desirable place for certain moneyed families to establish residence.

Before influential families began building palaces on Nob Hill, though, the Episcopal Diocese of California erected a substantial church building on the eastern slope. The cornerstone for Grace Church was laid by the bishop in 1860, and the building was consecrated in 1862. When the well-to-do families established themselves on Nob Hill, Grace Church played a significant role in San Francisco society.

The most prominent figures on Nob Hill were the Associates, also known as the Big Four. Collis P. Huntington, Mark Hopkins, Leland Stanford, and Charles Crocker were the founders of the Central Pacific Railroad. With land grants received by influencing a Republican Congress and administration (that of Abraham Lincoln), these magnates built the western portion of the transcontinental railway and amassed enormous personal fortunes in the process. The residences that they arranged to be built atop Nob Hill advertised the extent of their fortunes. Another man who had made his money in the West, James Clair Flood, would build a fifth grand house that would, in one way, best them all.

There was more to those times in Nob Hill, though, than luxury and glitter. Neighbors clashed, workers staged a dramatic protest, and society witnessed rebellion among its own. One daughter of a prominent family disappeared on the afternoon of her debut, apparently fleeing the prospect of marriage to the doltish son of family friends. The story goes that, in true San Francisco form, she took along her fabulous French ball gown, which was found on the body of a woman who died in humble circumstances in another western state years later. The woman's ghost is said to frequent Nob Hill to this day, though sightings have become increasingly rare.

From the 1870s to the early years of the 20th century, Nob Hill was a spectacular showcase. Magnificent residences sat sedately along California Street. Inside, they were furnished with exquisite treasures from around the world. The lives of those who lived on the hill were laced with romance, convenient arrangements, sorrow, grief, gaiety, corruption, and grace.

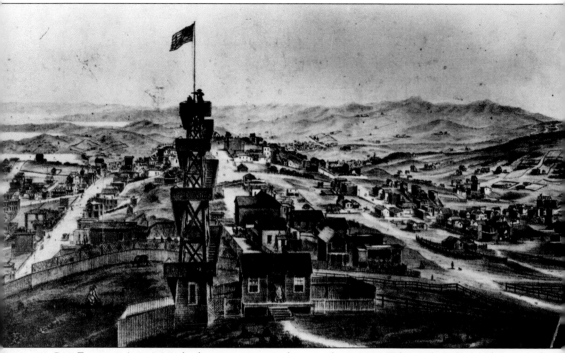

San Francisco's primary lookout point soon became known as Telegraph Hill. Looking south from that vantage point, Clay Street Hill can be seen. What would later become Nob Hill was a windswept collection of simple dwellings. It was Rincon Hill, in the northeastern part of the growing city, that was San Francisco's first tony neighborhood.

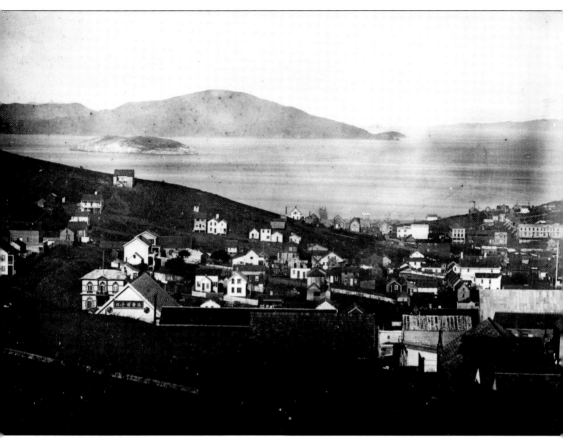

In 1853, four years after the Gold Rush began, this view from Nob Hill to the north shows modest houses dotting the hillside.

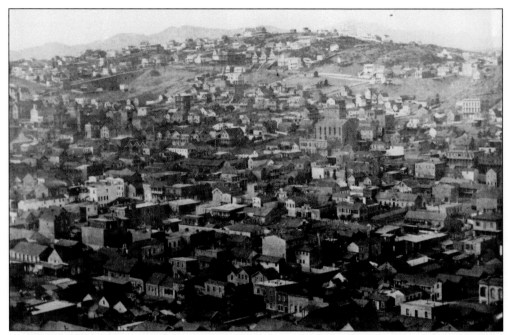

By 1860, dwellings were a bit closer together on the slopes of the hill, but steep grades prevented horses from drawing carriages and wagons to the top. Thus, Nob Hill remained only sparsely populated. (Society of California Pioneers.)

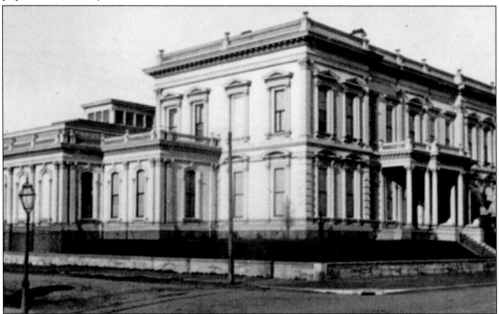

In 1872, the year before the Clay Street Hill Railroad cable car line opened, David D. Colton built this neoclassical residence on what would become the site of Huntington Park. Colton was sometimes referred to as the "Half" of the Big Four and a Half. The Big Four, or the Associates, as they called themselves, were the founders of the Central Pacific Railroad. In the aftermath of David Colton's death, his widow, Ellen White Colton, originally from Chicago, lost her shares in the railroad to the Big Four. The house eventually became one of Huntington's residences.

12

Collis Potter Huntington was born in Connecticut in 1821. An uneducated man, he followed the Gold Rush to Sacramento, where he met Mark Hopkins, born in Upstate New York in 1813. The two went into the hardware business together. The combination of Huntington's brashness and Hopkins's head for business would prove a dynamic one when they became two of the founders of the Central Pacific Railroad. Huntington was first married to Elizabeth Stoddard. In 1884, the year following his first wife's death, he married his mistress, Arabella, known as "Belle." Arabella, who was living as the wife of John Worsham, was 30 years younger than Huntington. After Collis Huntington's death, she married his nephew Henry Huntington. Elizabeth and Collis adopted her niece Clara Elizabeth Prentice, who grew up to marry Prince Francis Edward von Hatzfeldt, a German. Huntington spent much of his time on the East Coast, wheeling and dealing, especially with those who wielded power in the federal government. He died in 1900 at his camp in the Adirondacks. (Ron Henggeler.)

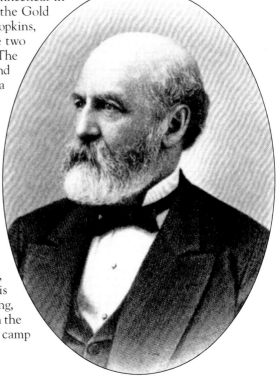

Catherine Arabella Duvall Yarrington Huntington, known as "Belle," has been described by at least one contemporary as "a young woman of uncommon beauty." Though some looked down on her because of her complex past, Arabella Huntington was an intelligent woman who studied art history and languages, becoming fluent in French. Her particular interests in religious art objects from the Middle Ages and the Renaissance, as well as paintings by the Old Masters, began a tradition in her family that has benefitted the Palace of the Legion of Honor, the Metropolitan Museum of Art, Yale University, and, of course, the Huntington Library. (The Nob Hill Association.)

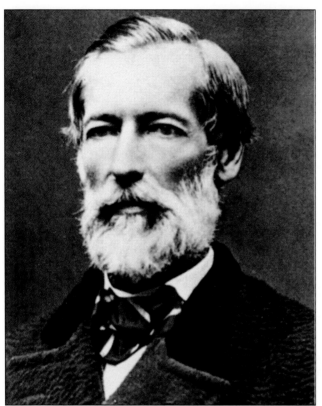

Mark Hopkins (1814–1878) entered into various business ventures in New York before journeying around Cape Horn to San Francisco in 1849. "Uncle Mark," the eldest of the Associates, was treasurer of the Central Pacific Railroad. (Ron Henggeler.)

The Hopkins palace was the grandest of the Nob Hill residences, but Hopkins never lived in the fantastic house at the southeast corner of California and Mason Streets. He died while on railroad business in Yuma, Arizona, shortly before the home was completed.

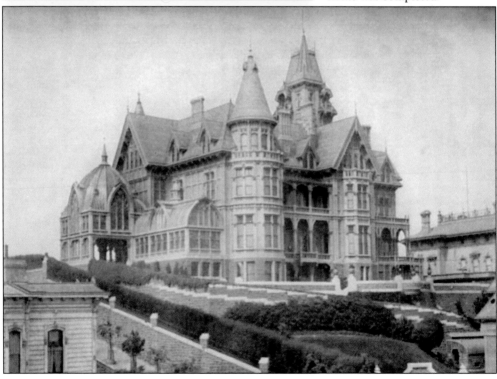

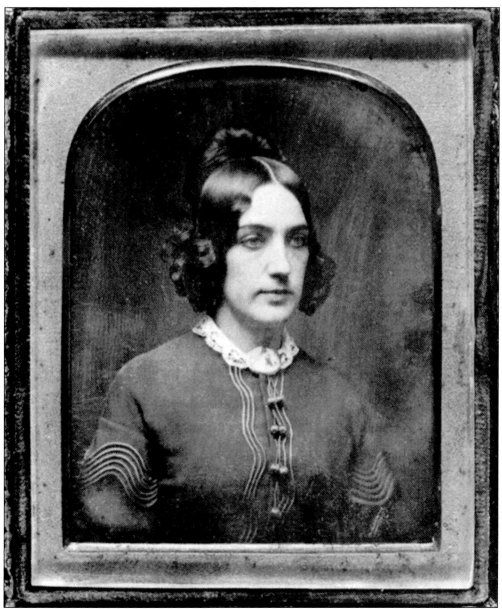

Hopkins's wife, Mary Sherwood Hopkins, did not remain long in the Victorian mansion on Nob Hill. After Mark Hopkins's death in 1878, Mary left San Francisco for New York and married interior decorator Edward T. Searles. Arthur T. Walker, thought by many historians to be Searles's lover, lived with Mary and Edward. From Massachusetts himself, Searles designed Mary's new home in Great Barrington, a stone edifice known as Searles Castle. Mary had adopted her housekeeper's adult son, Timothy Nolan, but had disinherited him. Upon Mary's death in 1891, Nolan sued Searles for part of the estate and received a portion of the holdings. Searles, however, retained the greater part of the legacy, some of which he later left to Arthur T. Walker. Searles donated the Nob Hill building and grounds to the San Francisco Art Association, since renamed the San Francisco Art Institute, located in North Beach.

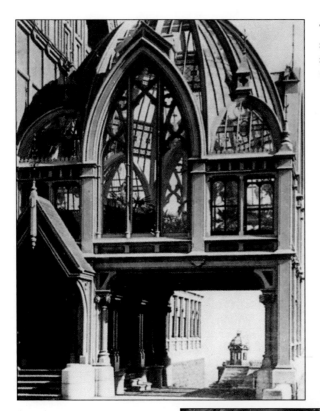

The Hopkins residence had a magnificent porte cochere, above which was a conservatory. (Ron Henggeler.)

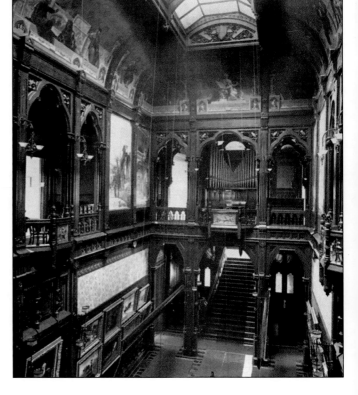

The interior was a vast collection of art and materials from all over the world. The staircase in the center of this photograph leads to the conservatory above the porte cochere. The pipe organ sits above the stairs, and the cords for controlling the skylight are visible. (Ron Henggeler.)

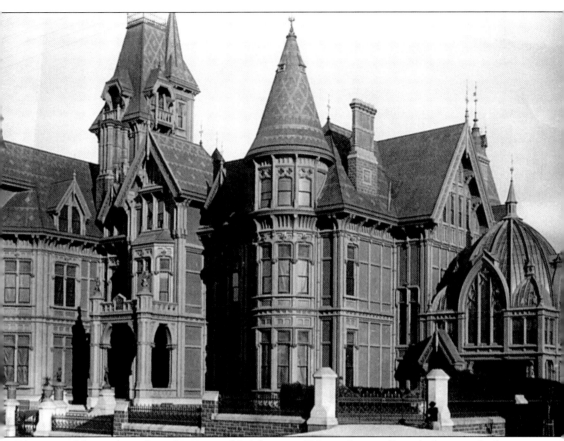

This view of the residence from the corner of California and Mason Streets offers a look at neo-Gothic details such as arched windows and quatrefoil ornamentation. The gateway in the foreground is situated where the front entrance of the Mark Hopkins Hotel is today. (Ron Henggeler.)

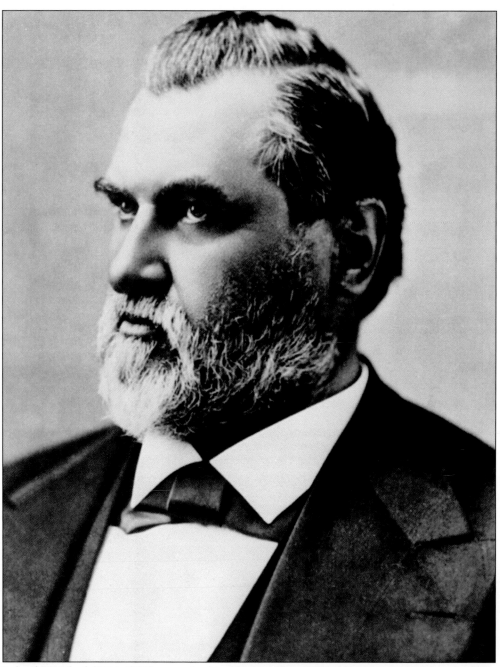

Leland Stanford (1824–1893) was raised in Upstate New York, where he studied law. In 1852, Stanford relocated to California, where he became a merchant, served as justice of the peace, and helped to organize the Sacramento Public Library system. In 1856, he brought his wife, Jane Elizabeth Lathrop, to San Francisco. The Stanfords ran a lucrative mercantile business. In 1861, the Central Pacific Railroad Company was incorporated, and Stanford was elected president. That same year, Stanford, active in the California Republican Party, was elected governor of the state, having lost a 1859 bid. Stanford held the office for only two years, but for the rest of his life he preferred to be referred to as "Governor." (Ron Henggeler.)

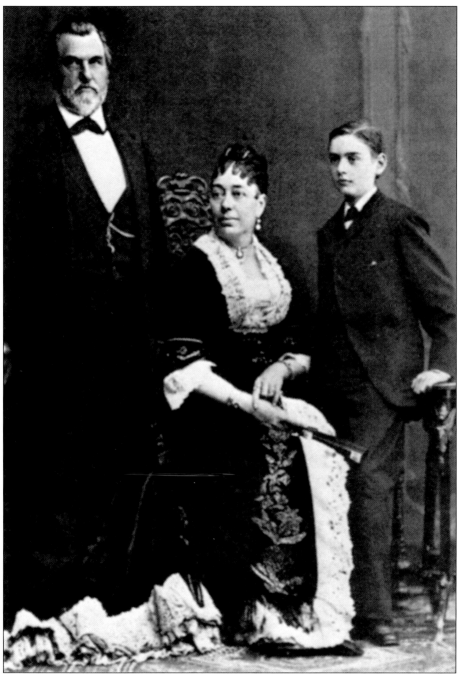

Amasa Leland Stanford and Jane Elizabeth Lathrop were married in Albany, New York, in 1850, where Stanford trained as a lawyer. Their one child, Leland Stanford Jr., was born to the couple well after they had established themselves in California in 1868. While the three were on a grand tour of Europe, Leland Jr. died from typhoid in Florence in 1884. In 1885, the Stanfords founded Stanford University in memory of their son. The elder Stanford died of heart failure at his home in Palo Alto in June 1893. Jane Stanford's death was the result of strychnine poisoning while she was staying on Oahu in 1905; the source of the strychnine remains a mystery. (Ron Henggeler.)

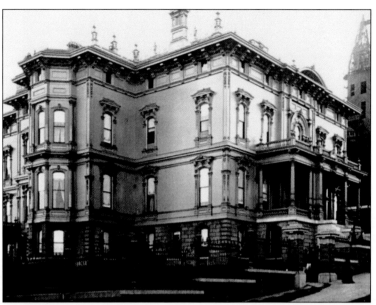

By 1875, the Stanfords had the wealth to build what was said to be the largest residence in California. This 1878 image depicts the ornate exterior of the home. The towers of Temple Emmanuel rise in the left background. The exterior of the Stanford place was almost spartan, however, compared to the fantastic Hopkins residence being built next door.

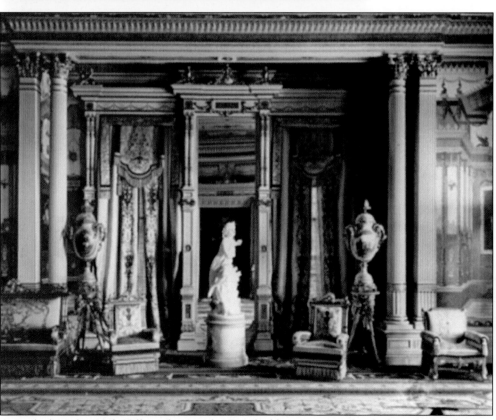

As with the other Nob Hill residences, the Stanford home was opulently furnished with items collected during extensive travels. Priceless carpets, elaborate draperies, and fabulous objets d'art adorn this room. The armchairs displayed with the sculpture and urns give a sense of the grand scale of the Stanford residence. (Ron Henggeler.)

Charles Crocker was born into modest circumstances in Troy, New York, in 1822 and lived most of his teenage years in Indiana, where he married Mary Ann Deming, the daughter of a sawmill owner. Crocker became president of Charles Crocker and Company, a subsidiary of the Central Pacific. As such, he was the supervisor of construction for the mammoth railroad project. (Ron Henggeler.)

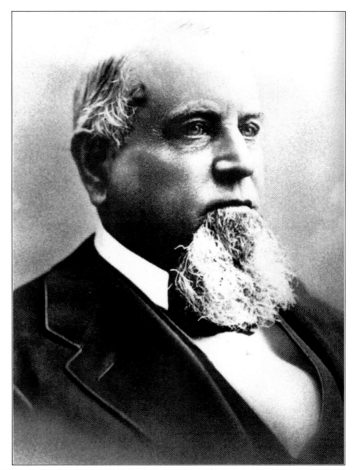

In the mid-1870s, as Leland Stanford and Mark Hopkins were having fantastic houses constructed on Nob Hill, Charles Crocker appears to have decided to attempt to best them. On the block across Taylor Street to the west of the Colton-Huntington mansion, Crocker built a substantial Victorian edifice (at left below).

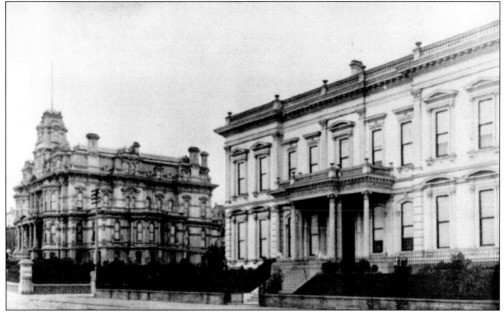

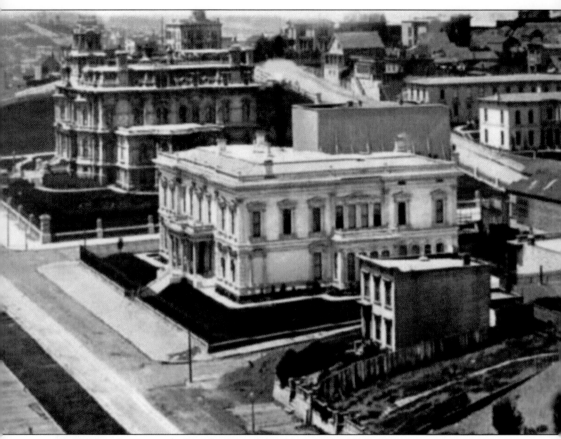

In 1855, nearly 17 years before the first of the showy Nob Hill residences appeared, Nicholas Yung and his wife had built an unassuming house at the corner of Taylor and Sacramento Streets. When Charles Crocker bought the adjoining lots, he attempted to purchase the Yungs' home in order to raze it. All attempts failed, and the result was what locals referred to as "Crocker's Crime": a 40-foot-tall spite fence surrounding the Yung house on three sides, cutting off sunlight and air on all sides except the northern exposure. Here the fence is visible on the other side of the Colton-Huntington place. It appears to be located at the rear of the Huntington property, but that is an illusion created by its situation partly blocking Taylor Street. In the end, Yung did sell to Crocker, who, as usual, got his way. (Ron Henggeler.)

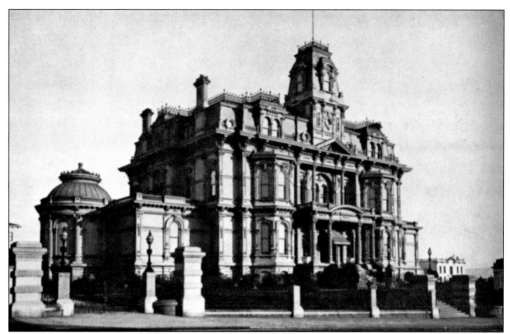

The imposing Charles Crocker residence was surrounded by a stone and iron fence, much of which is still there today.

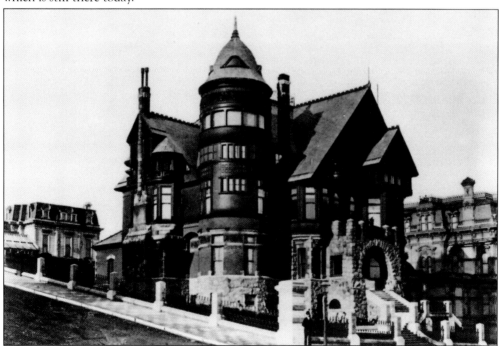

Charles Crocker also built a residence for his son, William H. Crocker, on the Nob Hill property. It stood at the corner of California and Jones Streets just up California from his parents' place. The home of William H. Crocker boasted a tower with a southwesterly view. W. H. Crocker became president of the Crocker Bank, which played a major role in financing the reconstruction of San Francisco in the aftermath of the 1906 earthquake and fire.

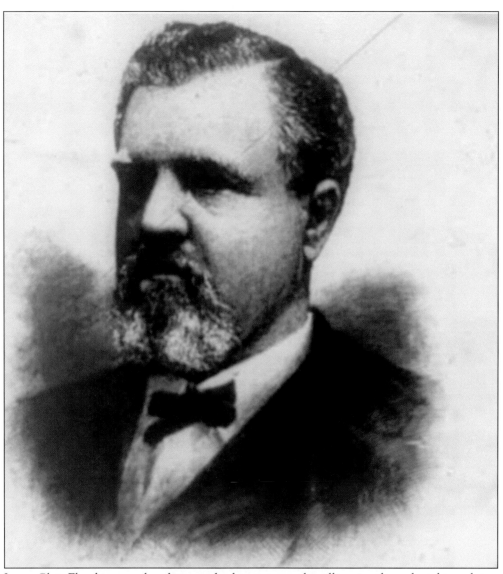

James Clair Flood was a saloonkeeper who became a multimillionaire through staking claims along the Comstock Lode in Nevada, which turned out to be one of the richest silver mines ever discovered. Flood was a forty-niner, and when he had made enough off gold to suit him, he went back East and took Mary Emma Leary as his wife. They returned to San Francisco in 1854, and in 1857 Flood went into the bar business with William S. O'Brien, who also became his partner in silver prospecting. Flood, O'Brien, James G. Fair, and John W. McKay formed the Consolidated Virginia Mining Company, which became a monopoly. When Flood died in 1888, he left an enormous estate. (Ron Henggeler.)

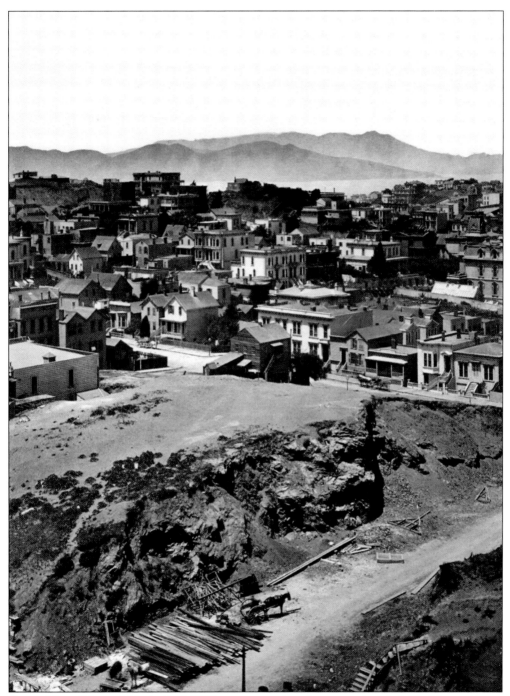

A panel from Edweard Muybridge's 1877 panorama taken from atop the Mark Hopkins residence shows excavations for the Flood mansion, which was completed in 1866. After the fashion of grand homes being built back East, Flood decided to build his home of Connecticut red sandstone that he had shipped around Cape Horn at great expense. The brownstone building is surrounded by an iron fence whose design is said to have been taken from a piece of lace fancied by Flood's wife, Mary.

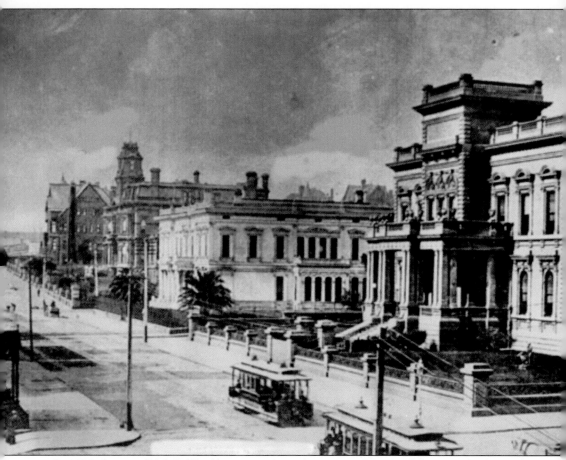

By 1886, the top of Nob Hill had been transformed into an architectural showcase for the opulence of a few wealthy San Franciscans. The cable car line provided access to the area, and the windy, craggy hilltop had been leveled to accommodate the huge houses. Westward along the north side of California Street from the former Mark Hopkins residence at California and Mason Streets stood the Flood, Colton-Huntington, and Crocker residences. The Flood residence would be the only Nob Hill mansion to survive the 1906 earthquake and fire. The house was gutted, but two wings were added in the reconstruction. The building now houses the Pacific-Union Club.

The Big Four and others who had amassed material wealth were not the only ones establishing a presence on Nob Hill. As the Gold Rush brought throngs of people to San Francisco from the eastern states, the Episcopal church in the area began to grow. William Ingraham Kip of New York was called as missionary bishop in 1853, and was elected bishop when the California diocese was created in 1856. Kip served in this post from 1857 until his death in 1893.

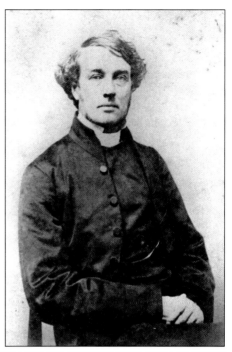

In December 1849, Grace Chapel, a small wooden building, opened its doors near Trinity Episcopal Church, in the midst of San Francisco. In 1860, the cornerstone was laid for a larger building on the eastern slope of Nob Hill, at Stockton and California Streets. Grace Church, called Grace Cathedral, was consecrated in 1862.

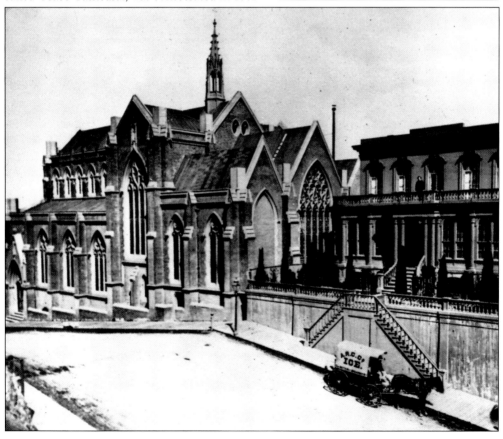

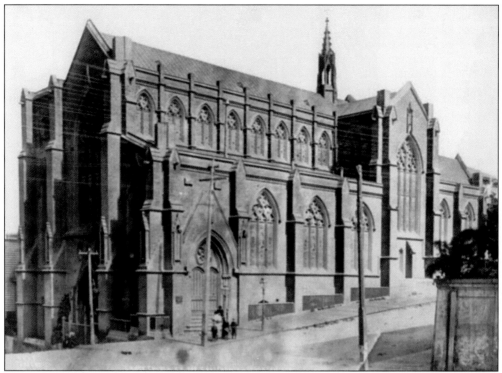

The first Nob Hill Grace Cathedral was a large, neo-Gothic, iron-framed building. On the vestry were some of the leaders of San Francisco society, with names such as Bancroft, Crocker, and Stanford.

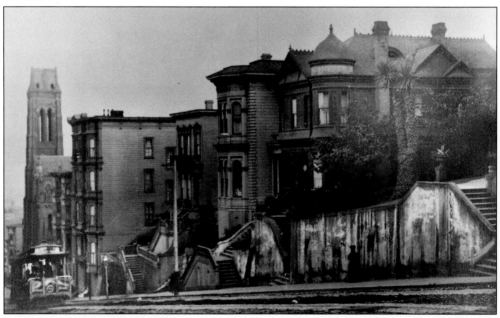

In 1890, the California Street Hill, on the eastern slope of Nob Hill, is alive with rumbling cable cars, attractive residences, two substantial churches, and a host of shopkeepers, residents, clergy, and visitors.

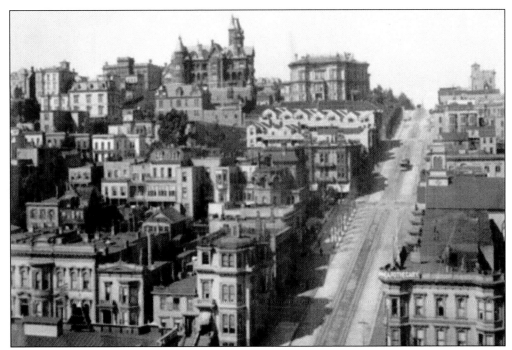

A view on Powell Street north from Union Square in 1902 shows the former Hopkins residence, with its distinctive towers, and the Stanford residence beside it. On the left is the Flood residence, the only building west of the Rockies made from Connecticut brownstone.

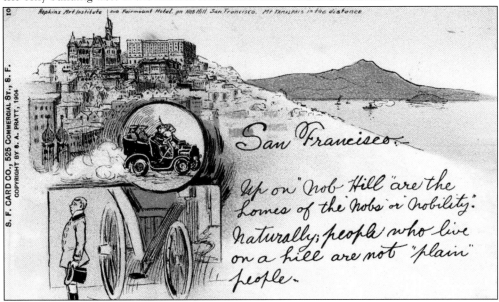

People were drawn by the glamour of Nob Hill. The 1904 sketch on this postcard appears to be based on the 1902 photograph, with the additions of the Fairmont Hotel, under construction in 1904, and, in the foreground, the towers of Temple Emmanuel. The former Hopkins residence is identified as "The Hopkins Art Institute." From fabulous private palaces to the palatial Fairmont Hotel to society weddings and funerals at the impressive Grace Church, Nob Hill was an alluring jewel to San Franciscans and visitors alike.

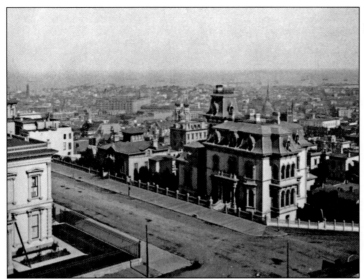

The Tobin residence sits on the southeast corner of California and Taylor Streets, where the Huntington Hotel is now. In the left foreground is the Huntington home. Visible just above the Tobin house is the old city hall dome. Across Taylor Street, just beyond the picture, is the Towne residence.

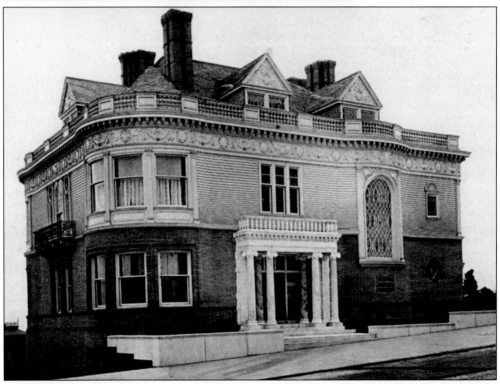

In the 50-odd years from the the Gold Rush to the 20th century, the Clay Street Hill had transformed from a windswept perch above San Francisco to Nob Hill, the center of wealth and power. The Alban Nelson Towne residence, at the southwest corner of California and Taylor Streets, was a graceful example of the era. In the so-called Bryn Mawr style, after homes built in the Philadelphia suburb, it features bay windows, intricate adornments beneath the dentils, beautiful fenestration on the dormer pediments, and detailed roofing. The Towne portico stands out for its balusters above Ionic columns. It would become a haunting symbol of the Great Earthquake and Fire. (Ron Henggeler.)

Two

DEVASTATION

The splendor of Nob Hill came crashing down in a matter of days in spring 1906. The Great Earthquake of 1906 occurred at 5:12 a.m. on Wednesday, April 18. An estimated 3,000 people lost their lives, and 25,000 thousand buildings in San Francisco were destroyed in the earthquake and fires that followed. The "Paris of the West" experienced devastating losses, and the ruins on Nob Hill were a shocking example of the results of the disaster. Like much of the rest of the city, Nob Hill experienced death and destruction, and the grand residences of Huntington, Crocker, Stanford, Hopkins, Flood, and Towne were destroyed, as were other homes. With the mansions, priceless collections of art and furnishings disappeared into the rubble. Almost nothing remained of the spectacular showcase that Nob Hill had become.

The impressive Fairmont Hotel was also a victim of the disaster. Though the exterior of the building remained relatively intact, the interior was destroyed by fire. When James Graham Fair, one of James C. Flood's partners in the great Comstock Load silver mining success, died in 1894, he left two daughters, Virginia and Tessie. As a tribute to their father, the Fair sisters set about building the imposing Fairmont Hotel in 1902. In April 1906, Tessie and Virginia Fair sold the completed hotel to brothers Herbert and Hartland Law. Just days later, disaster struck. The reopening of the Fairmont, exactly one year later, was a signal that San Francisco could do what was necessary to rebuild and to shine again. In the late spring 1908, Tessie Fair Oelrichs, who had been widowed, was back as the owner of the hotel she and her sister had built as a tribute to their father.

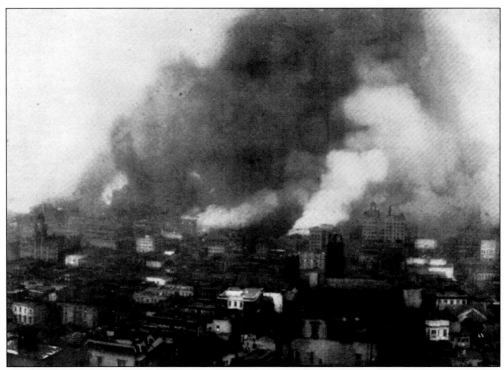

The conflagration that followed the earthquake raged for four days until desperate attempts were finally successful in putting it out.

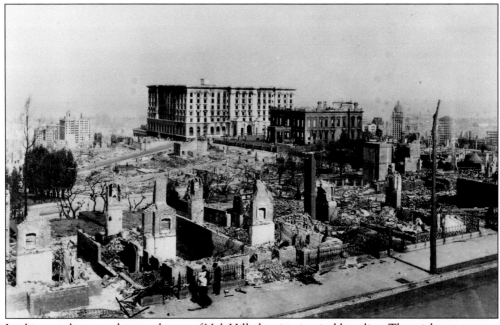

Looking southeastward across the top of Nob Hill, the view is mind-boggling. The mighty structures and their priceless furnishings have been destroyed. All that remains of most of the homes are the chimneys. Only the newly built Fairmont Hotel and the Connecticut sandstone walls of the Flood residence still stand, and both structures have been ravaged by fire.

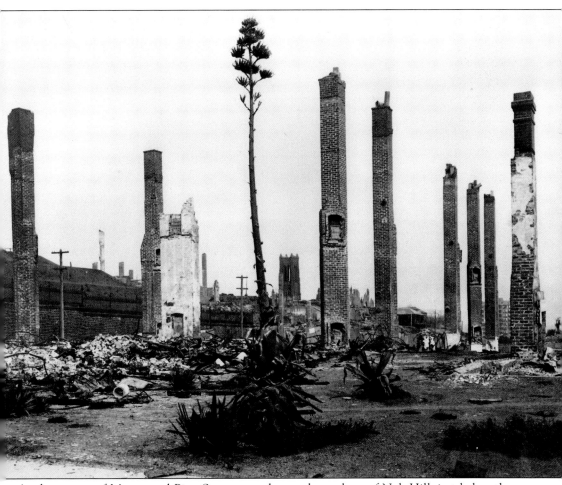

At the corner of Mason and Pine Streets, on the southern slope of Nob Hill, just below the Mark Hopkins residence, brick chimneys stand above the ruins of the houses they had been an integral part of.

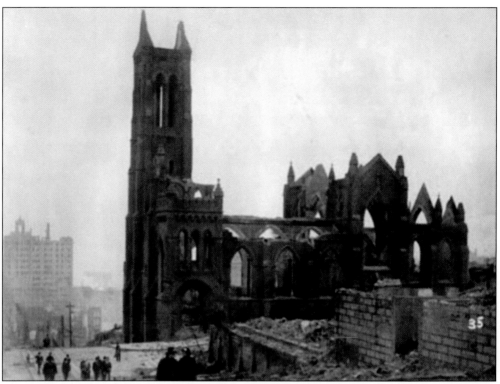

On the eastern slope of the hill, the building of Grace Church is in ruins.

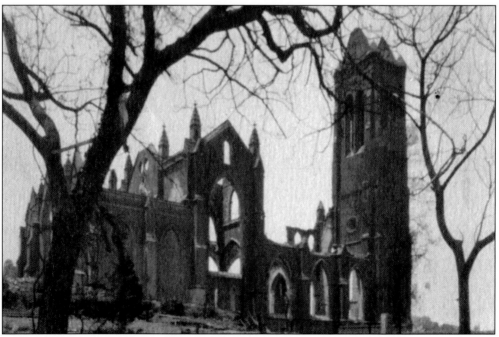

Framed by scorched branches, the cathedral building embodies the call for action to rebuild the city.

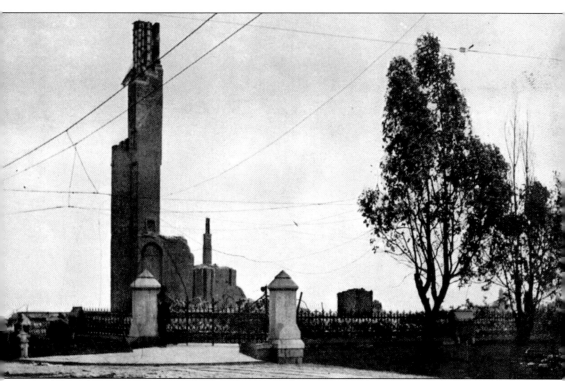

The label on the back of this photograph reads, "Mark Hopkin's [sic] Art Institute, Nob Hill, San Francisco. After The Earthquake & Fire Disaster, April 18, '06." This had been the California/Mason Street entrance to the spectacular Mark Hopkins residence. Visitors had arrived through this gate, their carriages pulling up beneath the enormous porte cochere that held a magnificent conservatory above.

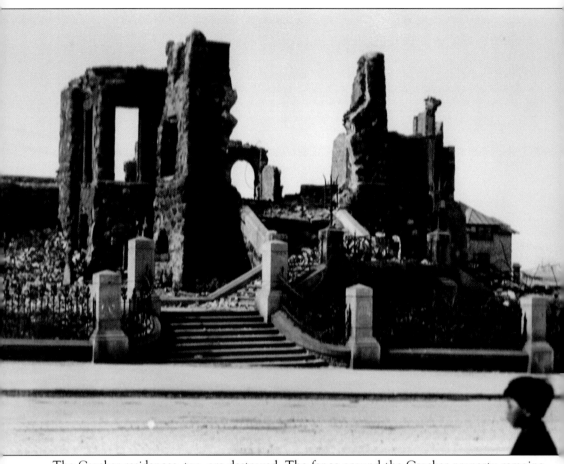

The Crocker residences, too, are destroyed. The fence around the Crocker property remains, though it suffered scorching. Such was intensity of the fire that some of the scorch marks are visible to the present day.

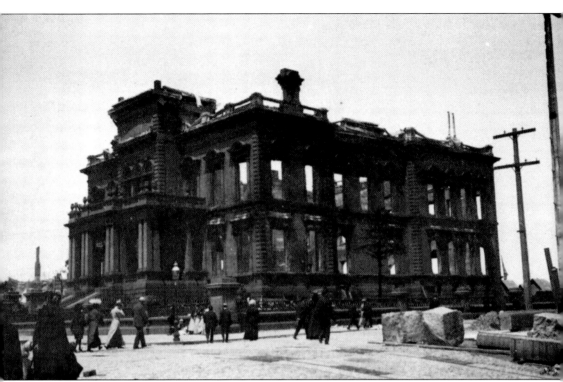

The only Connecticut sandstone west of the Mississippi in its day withstood the earthquake and fire, but the Flood residence is only a shell. The exterior of the building and the wrought-iron fence still stand.

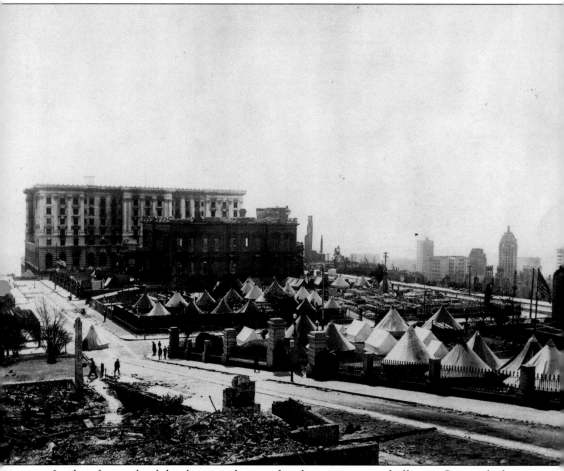

In the aftermath of the disaster, the city faced an enormous challenge. One such daunting endeavor was the Fairmont Hotel. It had been built by sisters Tessie and Virginia Fair to honor their late father, silver baron James G. Fair, who had passed away in 1894. The project began in 1902, but it became overwhelming to the Fairs, who sold it to brothers Herbert and Hartland Law in 1906 just days before the Great Earthquake and Conflagration. After the disaster, only the fire-damaged Fairmont Hotel and Flood residence stand on Nob Hill, alone except for the collections of tents that went up where grand residences had once been.

All that remains of the Towne mansion, at the corner of California and Taylor Streets, is the front portico. To the south, the ruins of city hall can be seen. For a while, the white marble columns stood fixed where they had been when everything around them had become rubble. Soon, the portico was removed and placed beside Lloyd Lake in Golden Gate Park. It is still there.

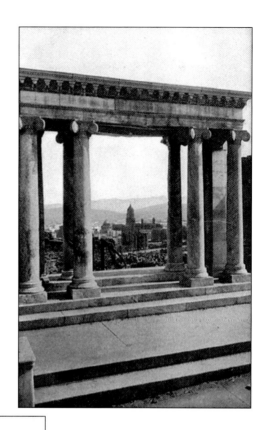

A PORTAL OF THE PAST

Like a phantom doorway, giving
On the Hall of Memory,
Stands the broken portal---living
Threshold of the Used-to-be.

Naught but space beyond—below it
Debris of the mansion's fall
At its side, pathetic, clinging
Remnants of the shattered wall.

Gone the wealth of pomp and splendor,
Treasures of the brush and loom;
Artistry of the smith and builder,
Mingled in their ashen doom.

The last rector of Grace Church, the Reverend David Evans, wrote this poem inspired by the Towne portal. In this verse, Evans, who was of Welsh descent, employs the ancient Welsh device of breathing life into inanimate objects, in this case the portal. He also immortalizes the material treasures that were held in those nine square blocks, using them as a metaphor for a vanished existence. The portal still sits beside Lloyd Lake and remains, as is the poem, a haunting reminder of the close of an age. They are also remembrances of the phenomenal reconstruction that followed.

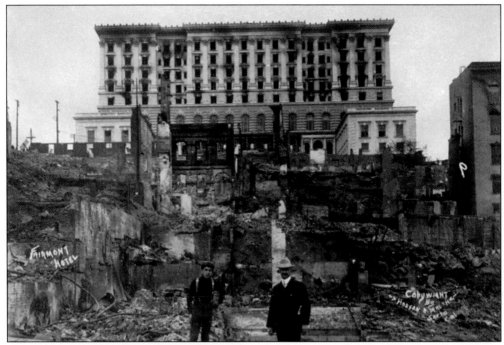

The Fairmont Hotel had been poised to open when the earthquake struck. Contemporary accounts describe the building high on Nob Hill as aglow with flames during the fire, its windows bursting. Here is the eastern facade, looking up from Powell Street.

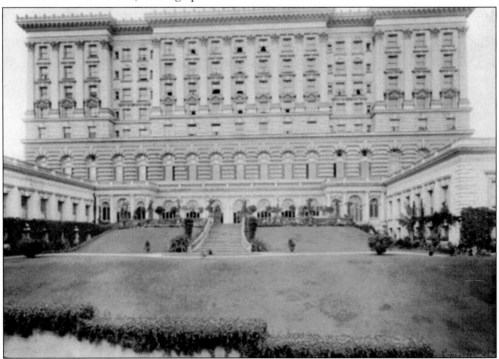

Exactly one year later, the hotel was ready to receive guests. The eastern facade and lawn were a testament to San Francisco's ability to rebound.

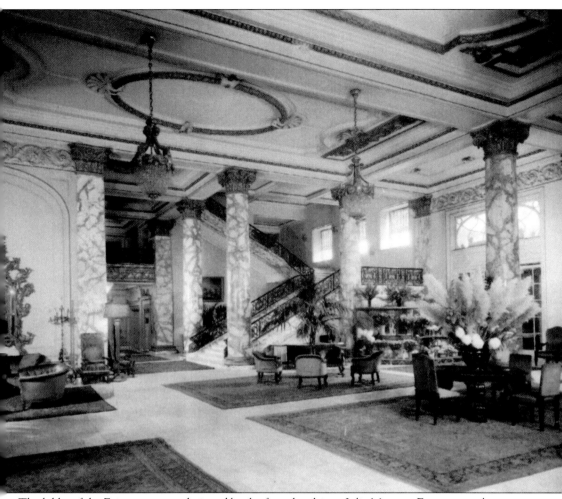

The lobby of the Fairmont was redesigned by the famed architect Julia Morgan. Enormous columns with Corinthian capitals, egg and dart cornices, and laurel garland moldings emphasized the neoclassical theme. At least one address on Nob Hill was ready to receive again.

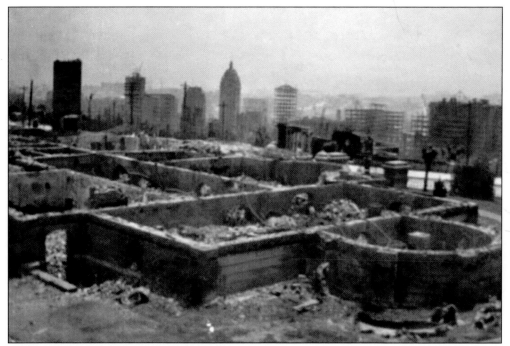

What was to become of other properties on the hill remained to be seen. Residents who had not already left, as had Mary Hopkins and the Huntingtons, were wary of rebuilding on the sites of such enormous loss. The ruins of one of the Crocker family homes are seen here in the foreground. A decision made by Crockers would have a significant impact on Nob Hill.

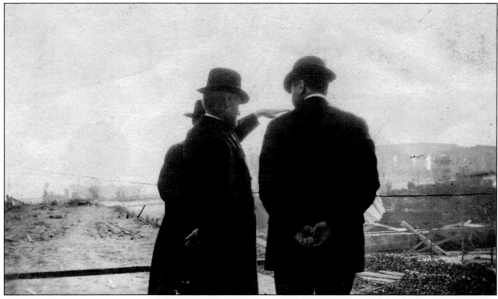

The Crockers were members of Grace Church, serving on the vestry. After the earthquake and fire, William H. Crocker, the son Charles Crocker, made a donation of the family property on Nob Hill to the Episcopal Diocese of California for the site of a cathedral. Bishop William Ford Nichols (left), the second Episcopal bishop of California, looks over the property with W. H. Crocker (right) around 1912.

Three

RESURRECTION

On the seal of the City and County of San Francisco, a phoenix rises from a ring of flames, symbolizing the resilience of the place and its people. Along with the rest of San Francisco, Nob Hill rose from the ashes of 1906 to make a glamorous and glorious new life.

Many factors determined the course of Nob Hill's future during reconstruction. Determination on the part of the Law brothers and the Fair sisters meant that the Fairmont Hotel would live up to its commitment to the city. The purchase of the Flood property by the Pacific-Union Club brought one of the oldest and most exclusive clubs in the United States to the top of the hill. Monumental real estate deals resulted in the Metropolitan Life Insurance Company headquarters and luxurious apartment buildings, some of which would later become fabled hotels. The generosity of William H. Crocker and his family made possible a great Episcopal cathedral. Arabella Huntington donated the land upon which the Huntington residence had stood, designating it for a public park.

From 1906 through the Roaring Twenties, Nob Hill transformed from merely an enclave of extreme wealth into a center of social activity and the heart of the Episcopal Diocese of California. In 1909, Metropolitan Life erected a large neoclassical building at Pine and Stockton Streets that is now the Ritz-Carlton. Hotels welcomed guests in grand style. Ned Greenway's cotillions brought debutantes and their families to the Fairmont. Fashionable residences attracted a tony crowd, and, after World War I, some of San Francisco's most prominent citizens were engaged in a campaign to raise the funds to erect a neo-Gothic cathedral.

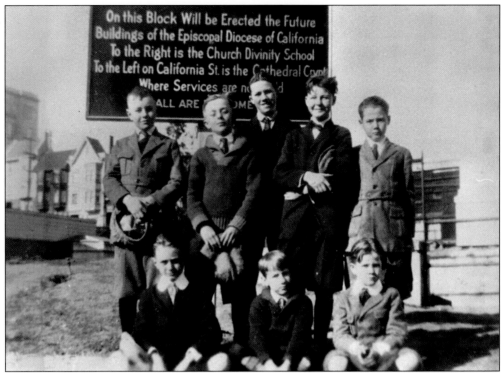

The Episcopal Diocese of California looked forward to building its home. Bishop Nichols laid the cornerstone for the cathedral in 1910, though ground-breaking did not occur until 1927. Pictured here from left to right are (sitting) three unidentified younger chums; (standing) Jack Nichols, Ogden Fields, Robert McPheum, Bill Proel, and Harold Williamson on the Taylor Street side of the former Crocker family property.

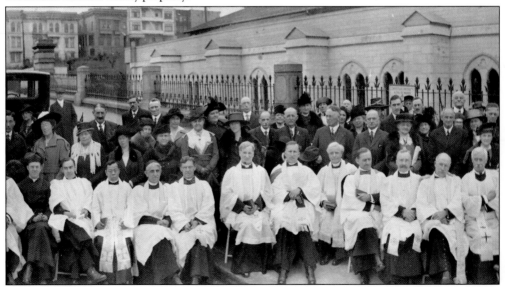

For the official group photograph of the 69th Diocesan Convention in 1919, clergy and other participants, as well as spouses, pose before the Founders Crypt of Grace Cathedral, on California Street.

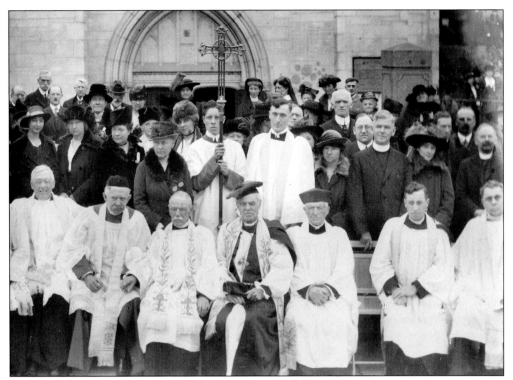

The Right Reverend William Ford Nichols, bishop of California, is seated in the first row, fourth from left. The Very Reverend Wilmer Gresham, dean of the cathedral, is standing third from left in the second row.

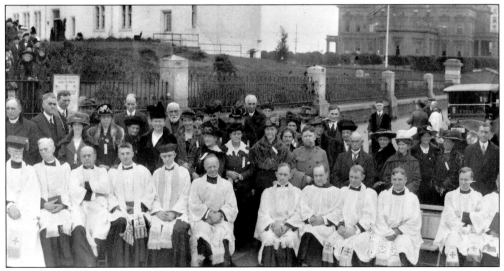

The Reverend James Otis Lincoln, assistant dean, and later dean emeritus, of the Church Divinity School of the Pacific, is seated at left, wearing a mortarboard. Nellie Olmsted Pitkin Lincoln, his wife, founded St. Dorothy's Rest in 1901 as the first free summer camp in California, serving sick and underprivileged children. St. Dorothy's Rest is the oldest continuously operating summer camp in California, with programs for all children and a special program for children with illnesses, and it is a year-round retreat center.

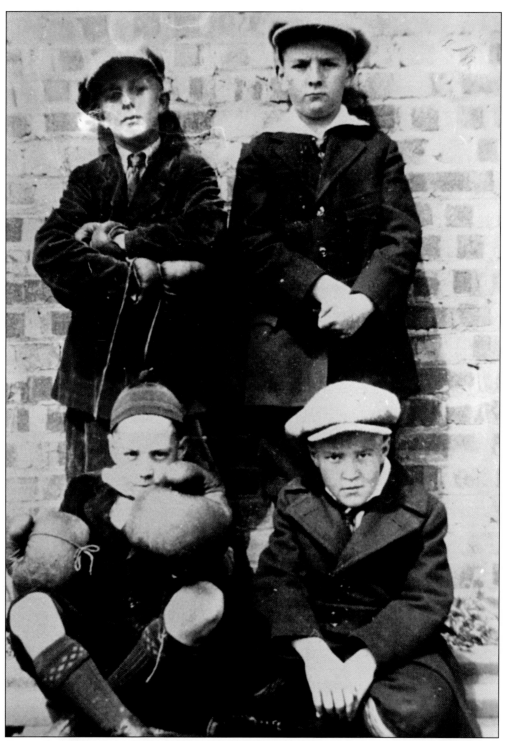

At another diocesan gathering, this one in 1922, pictured from left to right, (seated) George Williams and an unidentified friend; (standing) Jack Nichols, and Munroe Yunker try on a "tough guy" look.

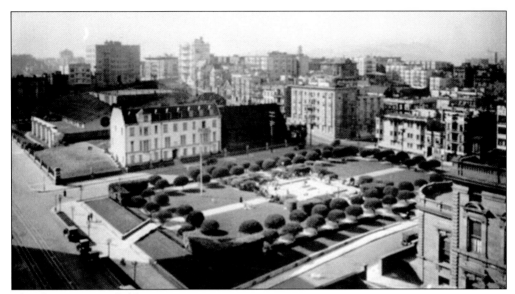

The above view, probably from atop the beaux arts 1001 California Street, shows, in the center, Huntington Park. Anabelle Huntington gave the land to the city in 1915 for the purpose of providing a park for all San Franciscans. The fence around the property was removed to a home in Atherton, where it reportedly remains to this day. The centerpiece of the park was a square sandbox for children to play in. The square box became a circle in 1928, and buildings were added to the west.

The first brick and steel high-rise structure west of the Mississippi, the Huntington Apartments were built on the site of the former Tobin residence, destroyed in 1906. Construction on the Weeks and Day–designed building began in 1922 and was completed in 1924.

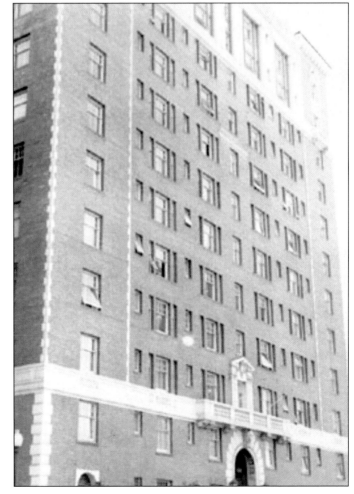

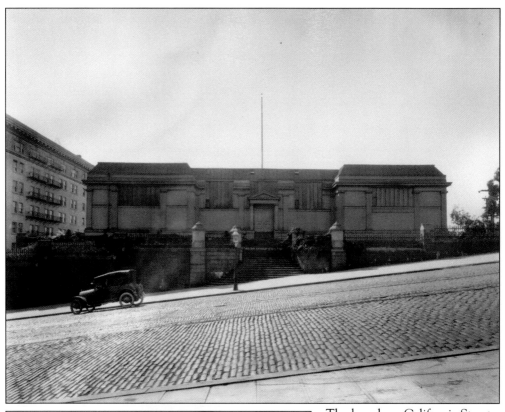

The low-slung California Street facade of the Mark Hopkins Art Institute stands in marked contrast to the towering grandeur of the home Hopkins had built on the site in the 1870s.

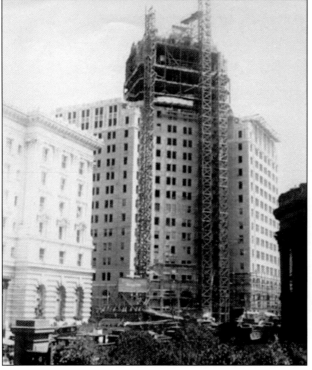

The Art Association building made way for the Mark Hopkins Hotel after George D. Smith, a mining engineer and real estate investor, purchased the land. The hotel opened in 1926.

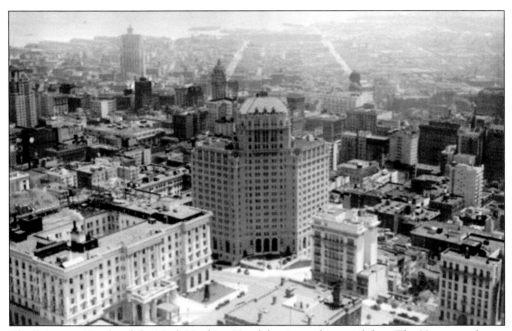

The Fairmont Hotel and the Mark Hopkins Hotel dominate this aerial shot. The Hearst residence, where Patricia Hearst came in 1976 to recuperate after her release from prison, is on the corner of Mason Street. The small building to the right is the Jewel Box. The rooftop corner (left foreground) is that of the luxurious Park Lane apartment building. (San Francisco Public Library.)

The renowned San Francisco architectural firm Weeks and Day designed the Mark Hopkins Hotel, a combination of French chateau and Spanish ornamentation. For the hotel's opening, Fresno-born artist Maynard Dixon, together with Frank von Sloun, painted nine 7-foot-high panels for the Room of the Dons banquet hall. The centerpiece is a gilded panel depicting Amazon queen Califa. (Mark Hopkins Intercontinental Hotel.)

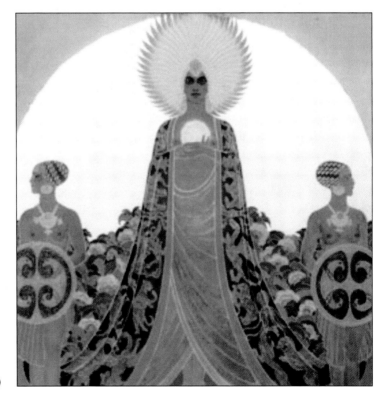

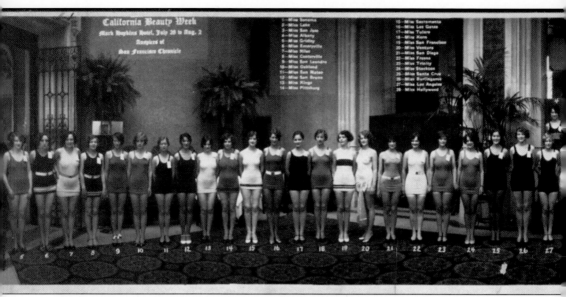

The Mark Hopkins was the locale for many social and civic events. In 1927, the hotel was the center of the *San Francisco Chronicle*'s Beauty Week, July 28–August 2. (Mark Hopkins

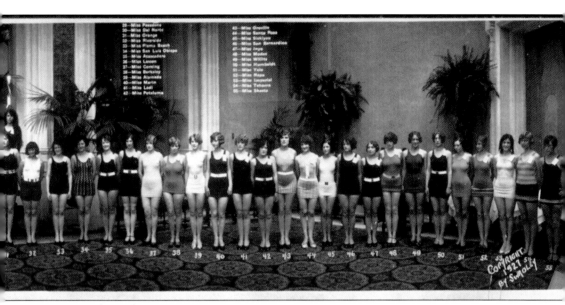

Intercontinental Hotel.

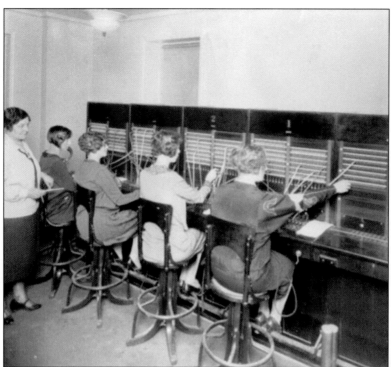

Behind the scenes, hotel operators were closely supervised to assure high quality service.

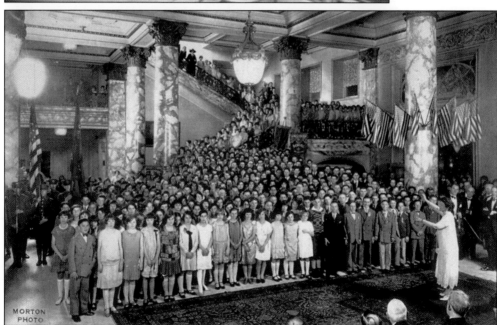

Across California Street, the Fairmont was in its second decade. Tessie Fair Oelrichs had hosted Teddy Roosevelt and President Taft. The Fairmont, having hosted every president since then, except George W. Bush, is known as the White House of the West. In 1926, the fabled penthouse was designed and constructed by John S. Drum, president of the American Trust Company. Berkeley professor Arthur Upham Pope, an expert on Persian art, decorated most of the fantastic interior. The elegant Julia Morgan-designed lobby was the site for social and civic gatherings.

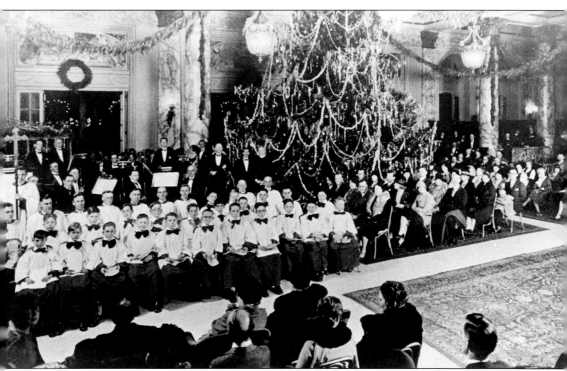

The sacred and the secular often coincide on Nob Hill, as in this 1920s Christmas concert. When Grace Cathedral consisted only of the Founders Crypt, hotels served as venues for events that would later take place in the cathedral building.

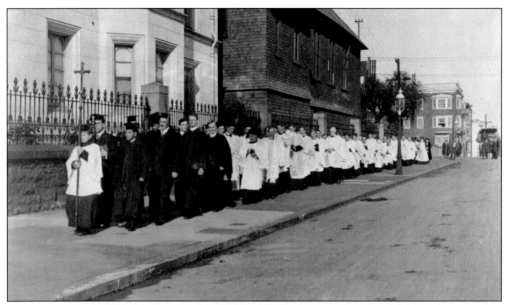

On the occasion of the ground-breaking for the Chapel of Grace, the first section of the cathedral to be built, this procession, led by the faculty of the Divinity School, makes its way past Diocesan House. The shingled building is the Divinity School.

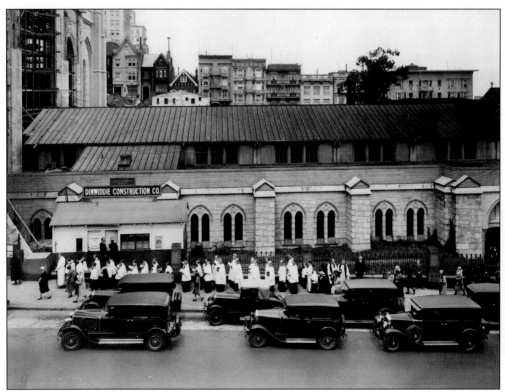

The procession reaches the Founders Crypt.

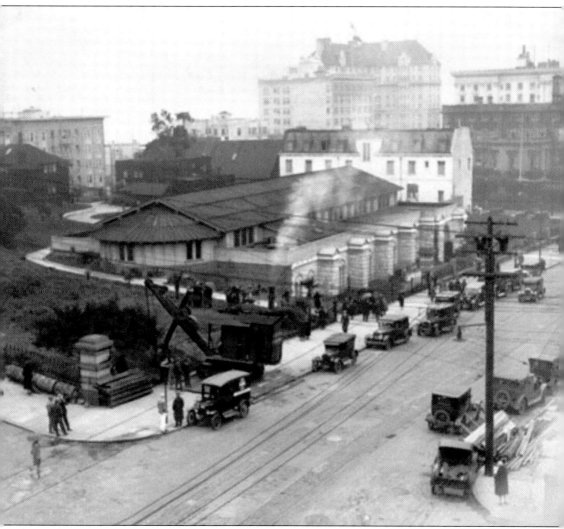

The northeast corner of California and Jones Streets, where the Chapel of Grace would be built, is in the foreground here. Beyond are the Divinity School and Diocesan House. Across Huntington Park sits the former Flood residence, by this time housing the Pacific-Union Club. The Fairmont Hotel is visible beyond that, and to the left in background is the newly constructed Brocklebank apartment building.

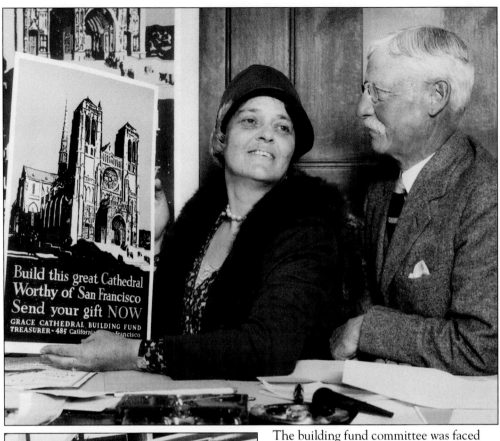

Build this great Cathedral
Worthy of San Francisco
Send your gift NOW
GRACE CATHEDRAL BUILDING FUND
TREASURER - 485 California ... Francisco

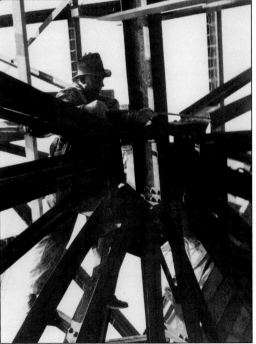

The building fund committee was faced with an enormous challenge. In May 1928, committee chairman J. L. Abbot and Mrs. Norman B. Livermore (née Caroline Sealy) posed with one of the building campaign posters. The architect, Lewis P. Hobart, who had designed Hillsborough estates and San Francisco office buildings, had done a cathedral tour in Europe. Seen here is his second design for the cathedral building.

Here a builder reinforces some of the vaulting.

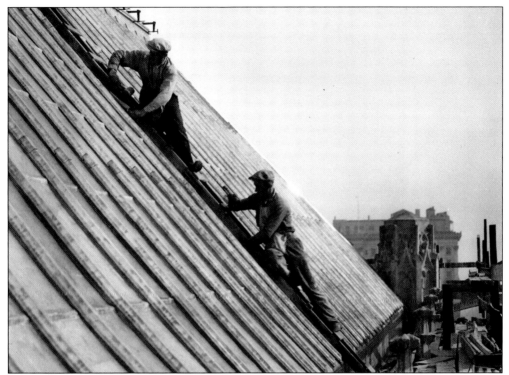

On November 22, 1929, craftsmen put lead on the roof of the Chapel of Grace.

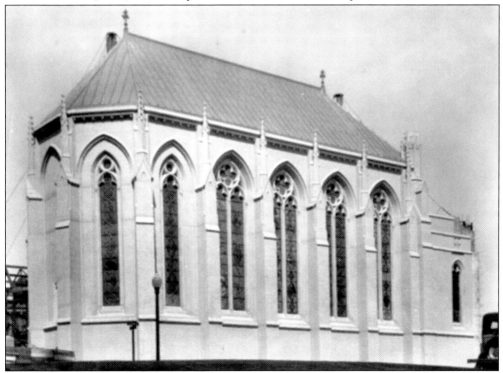

The Chapel of Grace was completed in 1929.

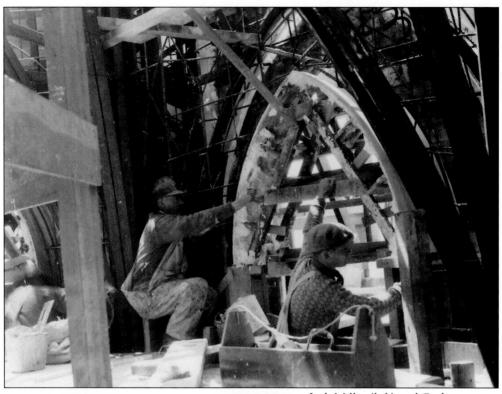

Jack Miller (left) and Carl Barry (right) were two of the craftsmen creating the cathedral building in the late 1920s.

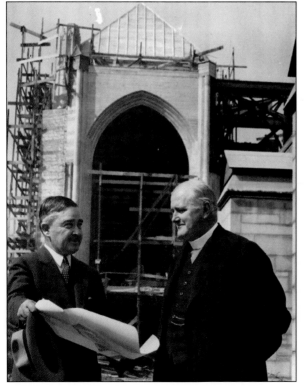

At the close of the 1920s, the construction of Grace Cathedral was underway. While visiting in October 1929, the bishop of Winchester, England, the Very Reverend Frank T. Woods (at right), toured the construction site with architect Lewis P. Hobart.

In 1930, as always, the Grace community looked forward to a glorious Easter Day.

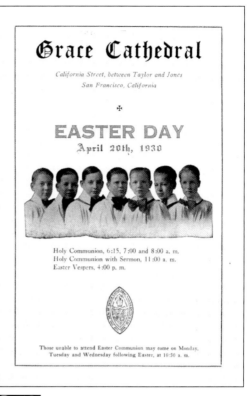

The late Easter in 1930 provided fair weather for the most important Sunday celebration of the ecclesiastical calendar.

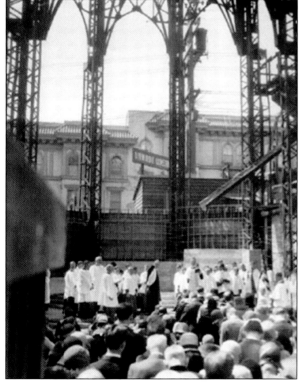

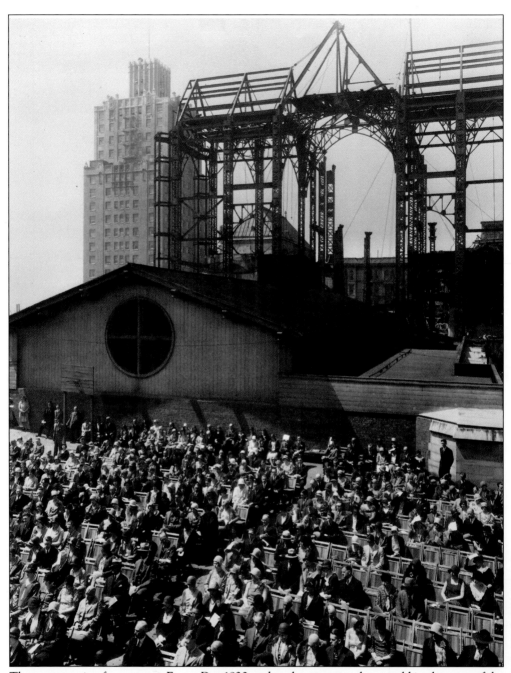

The congregation faces east on Easter Day 1930, rather than west, as they would in the nave of the future cathedral. Through the steel frame, the roof of the Chapel of Grace is visible. The newly completed Cathedral Apartments soar into the sky in the background. In Dashiell Hammett's *The Maltese Falcon*, published in 1929 (after having been serialized in *Black Mask* magazine), Brigid O'Shaunessy, "aka Miss Ruth Wonderly," stays at the Coronet Apartments before relocating to the St. Mark Hotel. Doormen at the Cathedral Apartments will sometimes point out Unit 1001, the corner place that many agree upon as O'Shaunessy's.

Four

DETERMINATION

The 1930s were eventful years, and in San Francisco, as is so often true in this legendary city, events were magnified. The stock market crash of 1929 brought financial ruin to some, while others flourished in creative ways. The ensuing Great Depression dashed the hopes of many people and also served as an inspiration. Labor unrest resulted in the establishment and strengthening of unions. The repeal of the 18th Amendment was, for some, cause for celebration in the midst of difficult times.

Nob Hill did not miss out on any of this. Indeed, the hill was often at the center of social and political issues and events of the day. By 1933, the building fund for Grace Cathedral was deeply affected, and construction had to be stopped. Despite this blow, however, hope continued, as a bell tower, as yet freestanding, was erected in the latter part of the decade. Through the generosity of Dr. Nathaniel T. Coulson, Nob Hill would have a carillon, whose 44 bells would become a focal point for the community. When Prohibition was repealed in 1933, the moment was marked by celebrations at Nob Hill hotels. During the labor strikes of 1937, employees of the Class A lodgings on Nob Hill picketed, and most of the guests vacated.

All the while, life went on. Each New Year's was rung in with formal parties at the hotels. The Grace Cathedral community continued to worship together and to welcome visitors. The Pacific-Union Club held fast. Children played in Huntington Park. Young people, who had no firsthand memory of the 1906 disaster, were coming of age in a city determined to forge ahead.

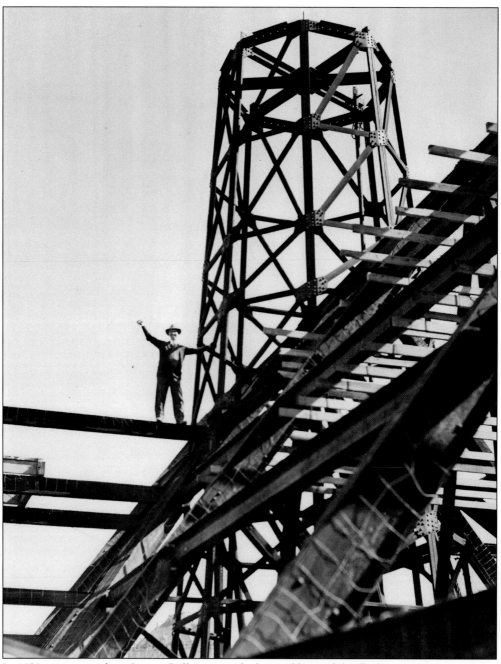

In 1930, superintendent George Ball poses with the steel base of the fleche, or spire.

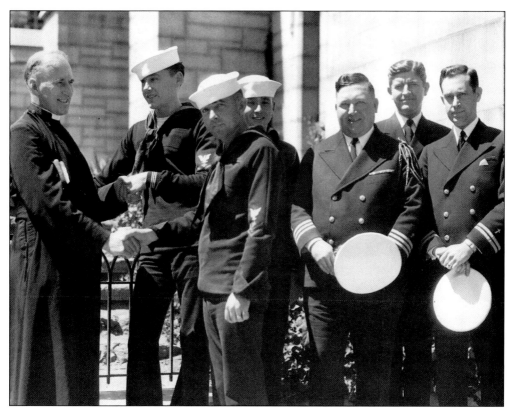

Archdeacon Porter (left) greets sailors at the Navy Welcome Service on August 24, 1930.

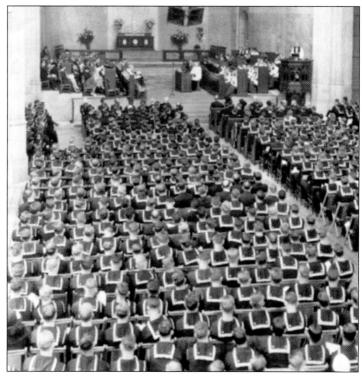

Sailors fill the pews in the nave at the Navy Welcome Service in 1930.

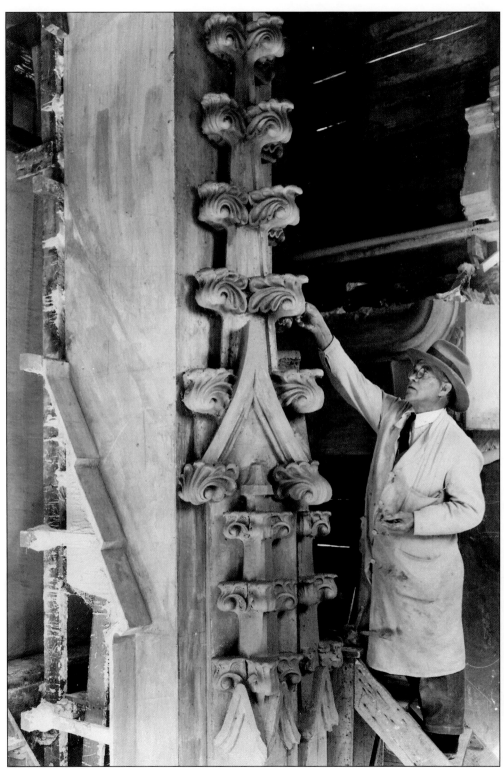

A. Cools inspects a model of a butterflies finial.

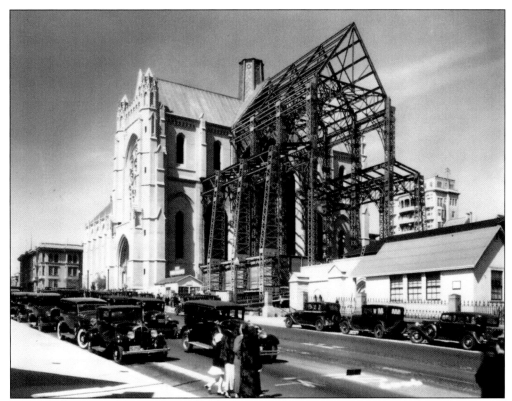

By 1932, the nave is beginning to take shape.

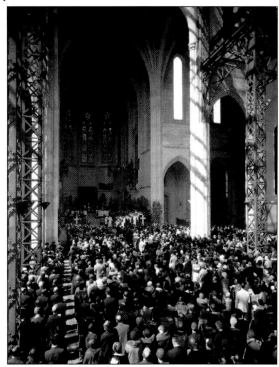

On May 30, 1932, the congregation attends
a service in the unfinished nave.

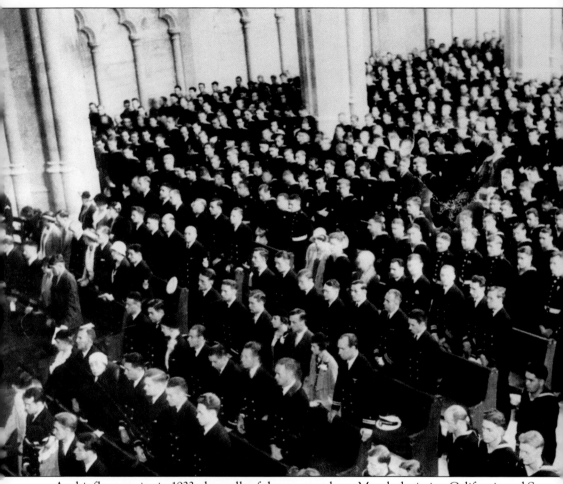

At this fleet service in 1933, the walls of the nave are bare. Murals depicting California and San Francisco history would be created later.

The year 1933 also saw the repeal of the 18th Amendment, the prohibition of the sale, manufacture, and transportation of alcohol, which had gone into effect on January 20, 1920. At the Mark Hopkins Hotel, Mary Richardson (right) is at the forefront of the celebration. (San Francisco Public Library.)

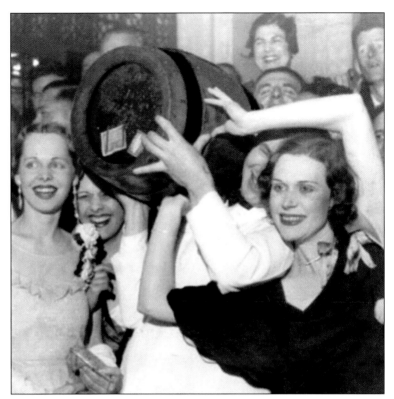

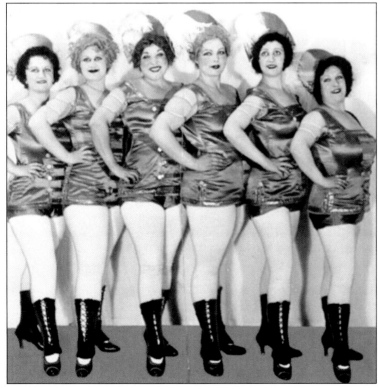

These performers display their voluptuousness at the Fairmont Hotel in 1934. (San Francisco Public Library.)

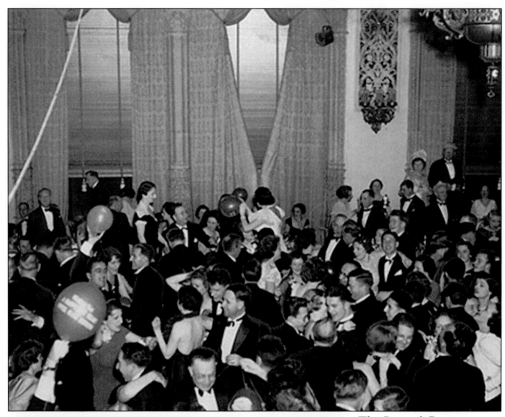

The Peacock Room
at the Mark Hopkins
Hotel is the place to be
to ring in the New Year,
1936. (Mark Hopkins
Intercontinental Hotel.)

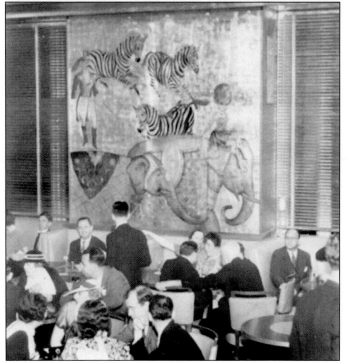

The Cirque Room at
the Fairmont is another
place to see and be
seen. It was the first
bar in San Francisco to
reopen after Prohibition.
(Fairmont Hotel.)

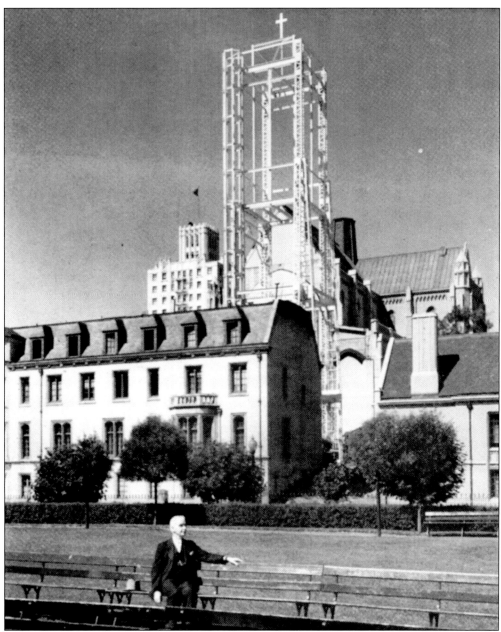

The Great Depression had a decided effect on the cathedral. Work on the building had been brought to a standstill in 1933. In the midst of economic devastation, however, a generous gift inspired the cathedral community. Dr. Nathaniel T. Coulson provided for the creation of the Singing Tower, the north tower, to be supplied with a 44-bell carillon. Coulson was born in 1853 in Penzance, Cornwall, England. At age 10, he was abandoned by his father and became a bonded servant in Lostwithiel, also in Cornwall. After serving in the Royal Navy, Coulson made his home in San Francisco, where he became a dentist and realtor. Dr. Coulson became quite wealthy, but met with financial ruin after the 1906 earthquake and fire. He regained his fortune, however, and established a park in Lostwithiel. Then, in the 1930s, he gave all his remaining wealth to the building of a bell tower for Grace Cathedral.

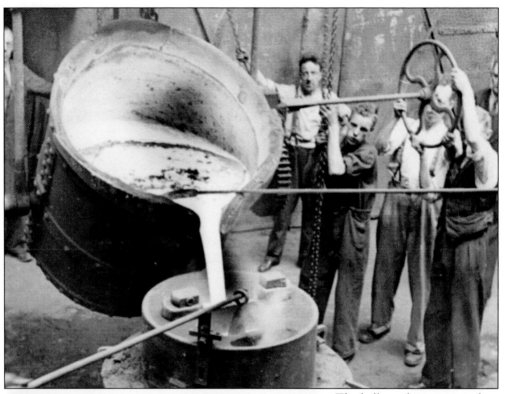

The bells are being cast and will be tuned at the Gillet and Johnston Foundry, Croydon, England, in 1938.

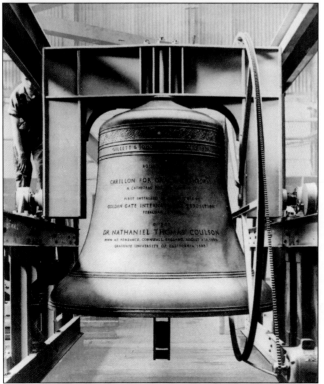

The six-ton bourdon bell, which is the heaviest and produces the lowest tone, is shown here at its unloading. It carries an inscription: "Bourdon Bell of Carillon for Grace Cathedral/A Cathedral for the Community/First Installed in Great Tower of/ Golden Gate International Exposition/February 16, 1939./Gift of/Dr. Nathaniel Thomas Coulston/Born at Penzance, Cornwall, England, August 8th, 1853/Graduate University of California 1885."

Dr. Coulson's Christmas card from 1938 joyfully anticipates the arrival of the bells at the exposition.

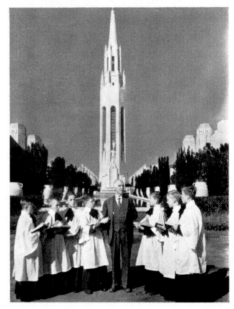

Dr. Nathaniel Thomas Coulson
With Choir Boys of Grace Cathedral
In Front of the Tower of the Sun
Golden Gate International Exposition

Christmas Greetings
Nathaniel Thomas Coulson

As indicated on the bourdon bell's inscription, the carillon was loaned to the Golden Gate International Exposition, on Treasure Island, and installed in the Tower of the Sun.

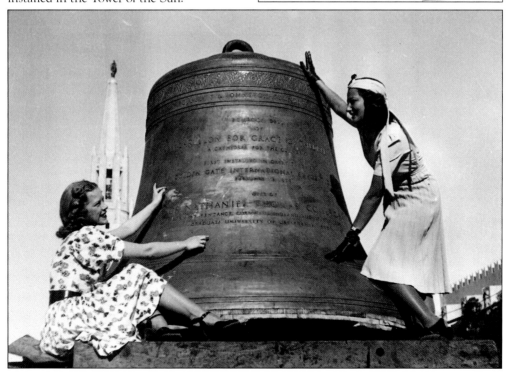

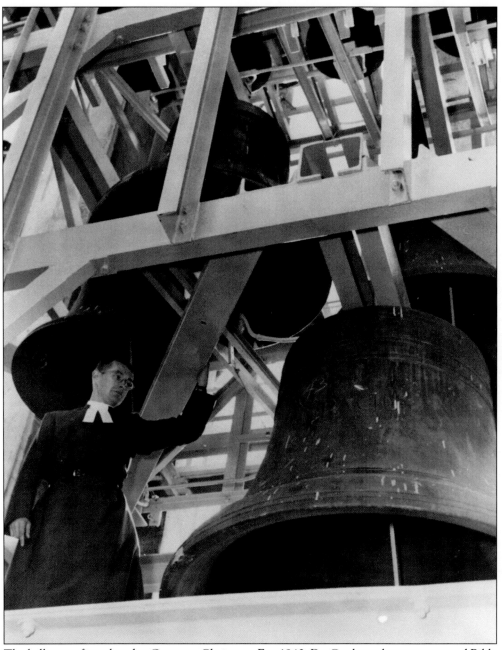

The bells were first played at Grace on Christmas Eve 1940. Dr. Coulson chose a name and Bible verse for each bell. The Peace Bell carries a text from Isaiah: "Nation shall not lift up sword against nation."

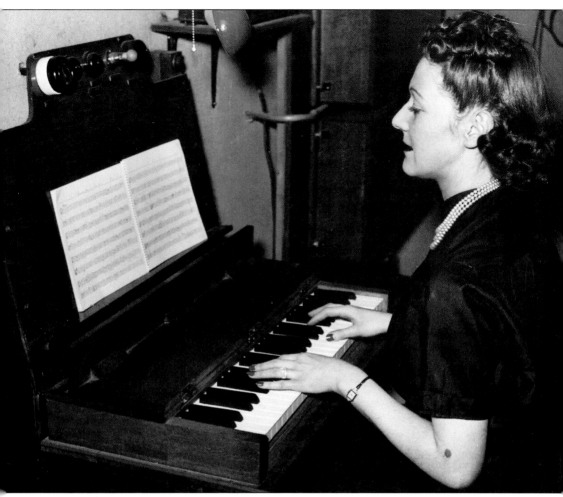

Though the bells chime the hours from 9:00 a.m. to 9:00 p.m. electronically, they can also be played from a keyboard console, as this unidentified woman is doing in the late 1940s. At the turn of the 21st century, the bells are most often played by Paul Goercke, Ph.D.

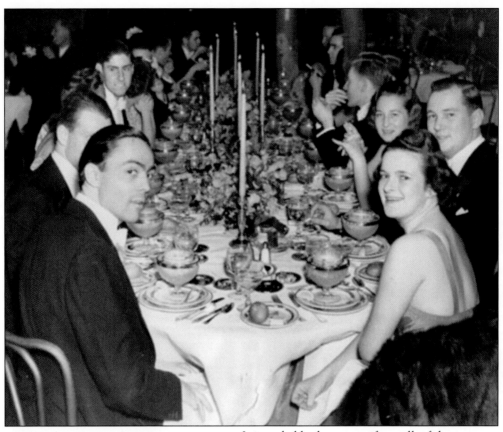

It is probable that most, if not all, of these fashionable young people at a dinner party at the Mark Hopkins in 1939 also attended the Golden Gate International Exposition and heard Dr. Coulson's bells ring out from the Tower of the Sun.

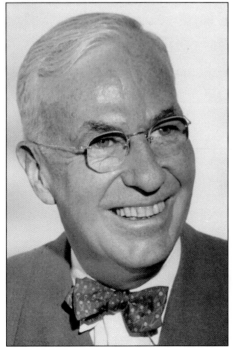

Across California Street from the Mark Hopkins, elegance and more abounded at the Fairmont. When George Smith (left), who also owned the Mark Hopkins, purchased the Fairmont in 1924, he added an indoor pool, the Fairmont Plunge. (The Fairmont Hotel.)

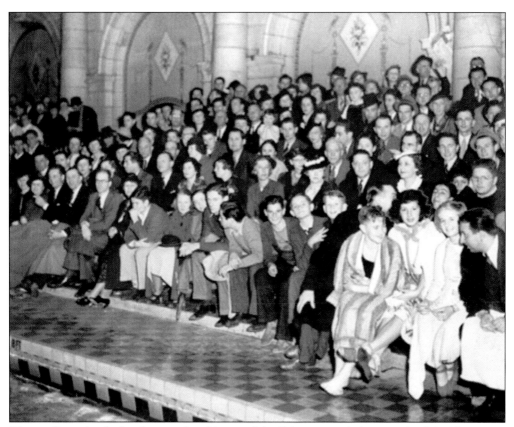

The pool's setting befits the grand ambience of the Fairmont and gives an air of significance to this competition on April Fools' Day, 1937. (San Francisco Public Library.)

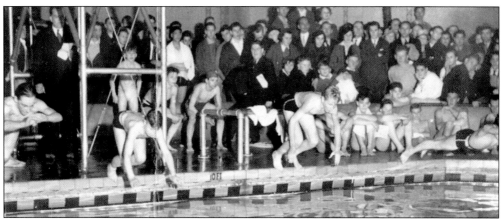

Competitions at the Plunge were well attended. Pictured from left to right, swimmers Philip Little, Robert Arnold, Carter Anderson, and Dave Hohnson are at the center of attention here. Later, when East Coast businessman Benjamin Swig purchased the Fairmont after World War II, the Plunge was converted to the SS *Tonga* and then the Tonga Room, where patrons experience South Seas flavor, complete with intermittent "thunderstorms." The dance floor of the Tonga Room was actually originally the deck of a tall ship, the SS *Forrester*, that sailed the South Seas out of San Francisco. (San Francisco Public Library.)

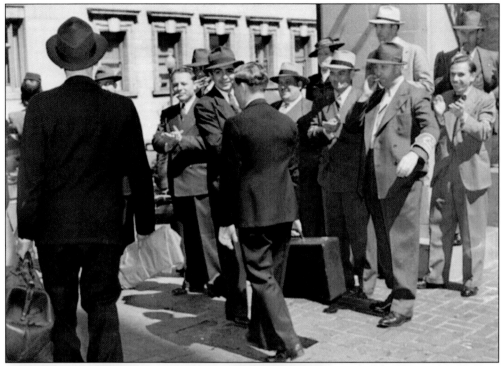

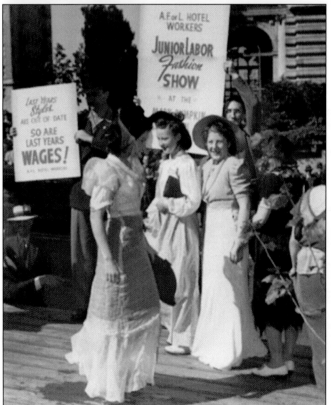

Hotels had been major sites during the strike of 1937. At the Fairmont, the Plunge was closed; and at the Mark Hopkins, the elevator was being operated at one point by none other than owner George Smith. After 87 days, hotel owners went to the bargaining table with labor. The 1937 strike set a precedent for future labor actions, such as the 1941 strike. Strikers cheered as fellow workers joined them on the picket lines. (San Francisco Public Library.)

Nob Hill has been the locale for Junior League fashion shows through the years, usually in a hotel banquet room. This Junior Labor Fashion Show of 1941, which was put on during the strike, had a bit of a twist to it. (San Francisco Public Library.)

From the roof of the Fairmont, the pitched roof of the stately Brocklebank is just across Sacramento Street, and the upper floors of the Park Lane are a stones throw across the intersection of Mason and Sacramento Streets. (San Francisco Public Library.)

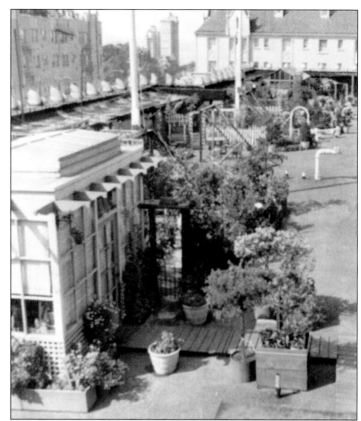

On a March day in 1940, with no picket lines below and no immediate threat of war, Mrs. Douglas Crane was photographed in the roof garden of the Fairmont's famous penthouse. Mr. and Mrs. Douglas B. Crane were listed among the "permanent guests" of the Fairmont. (San Francisco Public Library.)

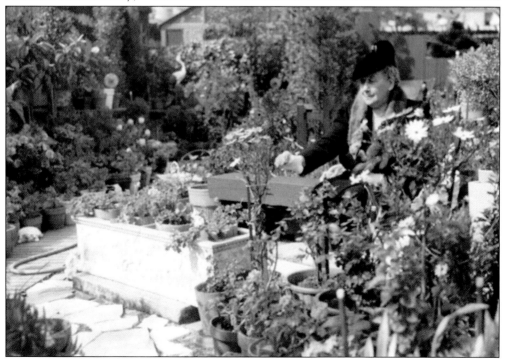

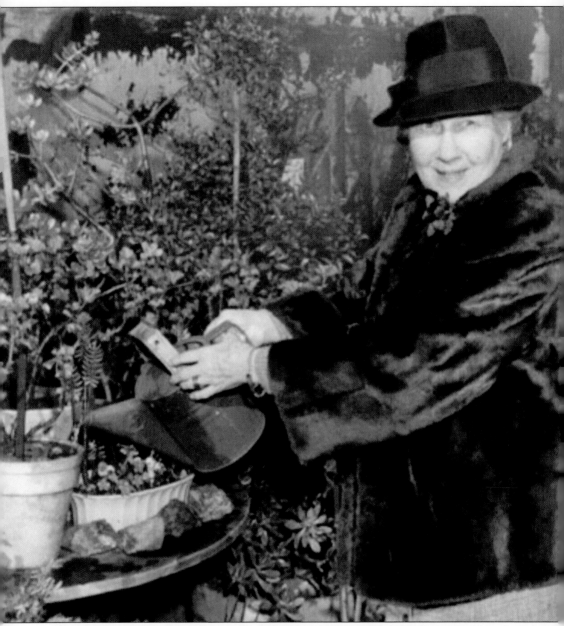

Having removed her gloves (but certainly not her fur) to wield a watering can, Crane's aspect recalls the calm optimism often needed to cope during the Depression and the Second World War. (San Francisco Public Library.)

Five

DEVOTION AND COMPLETION

On Sunday, December 7, 1941, the attack on Pearl Harbor, Hawaii, precipitated America's involvement in World War II, which had begun in Europe in 1939. Young men from across the nation answered the call. Many a wife and sweetheart saw her or his soldier deployed from San Francisco. On Nob Hill, many said farewell at the Top of the Mark, at the Mark Hopkins Hotel. Prayers and services at Grace Cathedral supported "our boys" overseas and efforts at home.

The Huntington Apartments became the Huntington Hotel, beginning a life of discreet luxury. Following the war, the Garden Room at the Fairmont, was the site for the drafting of the Charter of the United Nations. In the 1950s, the Fontana delle Tartargue was installed at Huntington Park, and the Masonic Temple was erected. The arrival of Bishop Pike foreshadowed the social tumult of the decade to come.

During the 1960s, Grace Cathedral celebrated the consecration of the cathedral building, and illustrious visitors came to join the celebration. By the early 1970s, when Det. Mike Stone (Karl Malden) and Insp. Steve Keller (Michael Douglas) investigated a fictional homicide at the Mark Hopkins and a later one at the Fairmont (with the Brocklebank used as that hotel's exterior) on the television show *The Streets of San Francsico,* Nob Hill's enduring style was being stretched to its limits by a rapidly changing society.

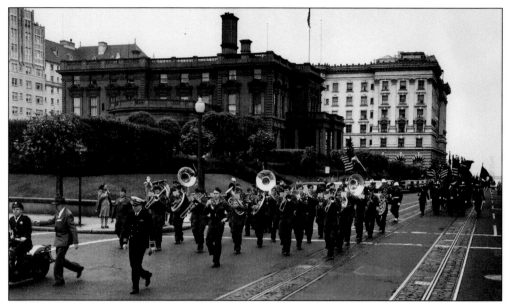

This parade makes its way west on California Street. The tall hedges are at Huntington Park. The Fairmont is behind the old Flood mansion, now home of the Pacific-Union Club. The flag atop the building is at full staff, indicating that none of the club's members has passed away recently. Visible beyond the club building are the Brocklebank and the Park Lane (to the west).

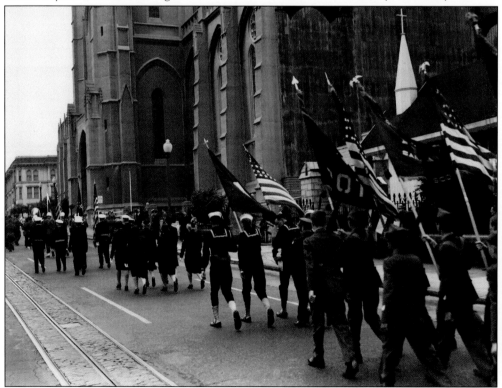

Continuing west on California Street, the parade passes the barrier that marks where construction on the nave of Grace Cathedral has left off.

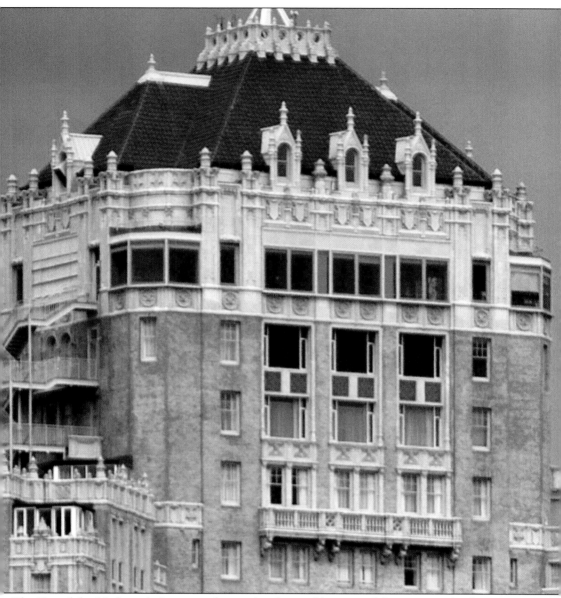

The Top of the Mark, with dancing, a bar, and unforgettable views of the city, was the favorite spot for officers to bid farewell before shipping out to the Pacific. Families went to the towering Mark Hopkins to watch servicemen's ships depart and return beneath the Golden Gate Bridge.

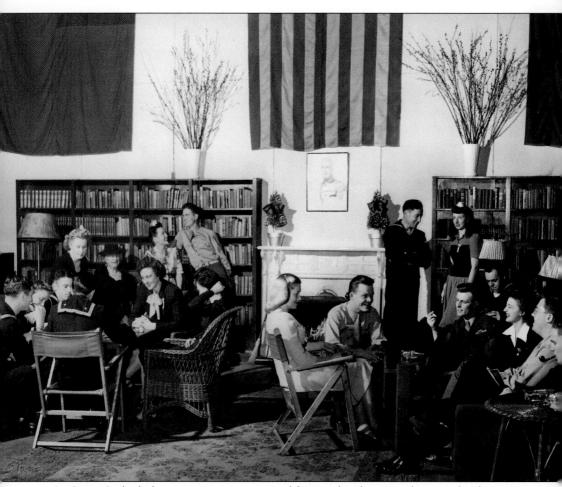

At Grace Cathedral, servicemen were received for social gatherings, always under the caring eye of a chaperone.

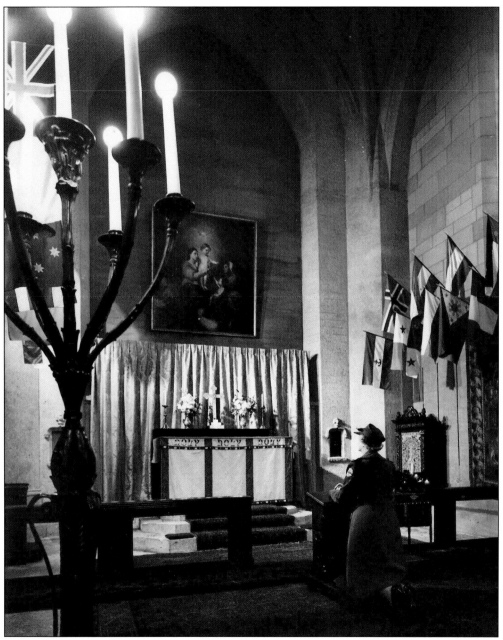

A clergy wife is seen here kneeling in prayer in Grace Cathedral's Chapel of Intercession, later renamed Chapel of the Nativity. Her uniform indicates that she was actively doing her part in the war effort.

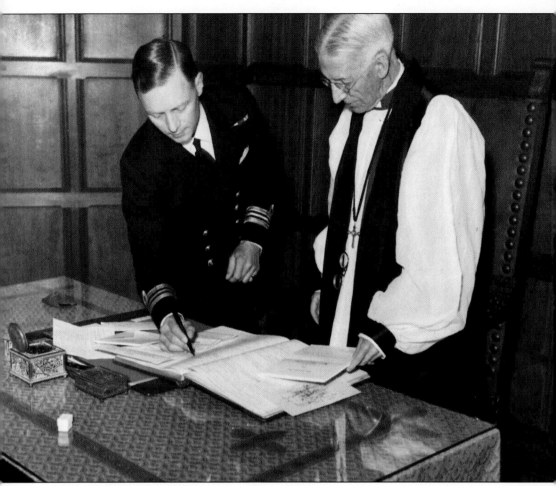

Ambrose Maynard Dudley Lampen, who had a 32-year career in the Royal Navy, earned the Distinguished Service Cross for his significant contribution to the Allied Forces' successful 1944 Normandy D-Day invasion. He is seen here signing the register on the occasion of his wedding in 1945 to Elizabeth "Betty" Grubb, a fourth-generation San Franciscan, in the Chapel of Grace. Ambrose Lampen held the office of cathedral bursar and was superintendent of buildings and grounds. He was installed as Grace Cathedral's first lay canon in 1966. Canon Lampen died in February 2010, at age 99.

Canon Crane, later bishop of Indianapolis, performed the baptism for his own child. Hats, gloves, and the proud and happy expressions of his mother, his mother-in-law, and, of course, his wife complete the picture on the sunny steps of Grace Cathedral.

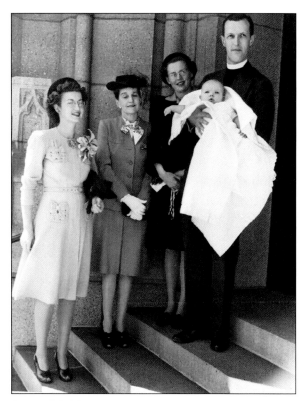

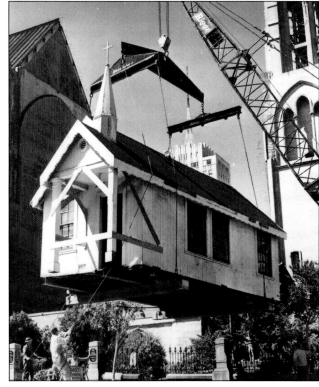

The Wayside Chapel of St. Francis, opened in 1945, attracted servicemen and was the site of many marriages.

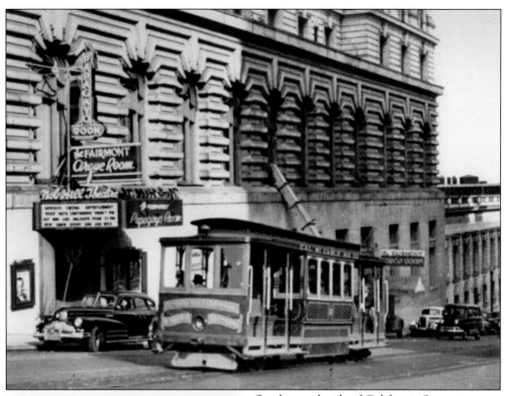

On the north side of California Street, in the Fairmont Hotel building, the Nob Hill Theatre (1944–1964) offered a respite from daily concerns. The California Street cable car line extended out to Presidio Avenue then. (San Francisco Public Library.)

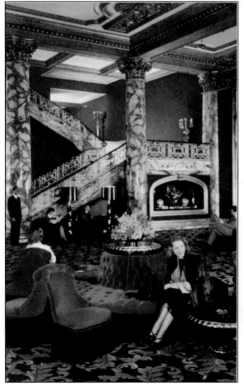

The Depression years had been unkind to the Fairmont Hotel, and the Second World War put things in a holding pattern. However, Benjamin Swig's purchased of the hotel and the Fairmont's role as the location of the drafting of the United Nations charter brought the hotel a much-needed boost. The icing on the cake was the securing of popular designer Dorothy Draper to redo the public areas of the building. (The Fairmont Hotel.)

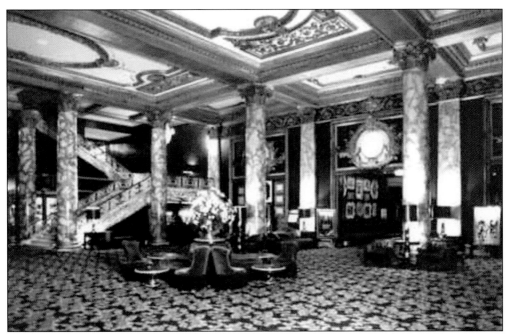

Guided by a sense of roguish charm and adventure, which she associated with both the Gold Rush and San Francisco itself, the designer worked in various shades of red combined with black and gold. The "Draper Touch" created a lush palace, which proved to be a draw for many, including royalty and heads of state. Draper's Venetian Room became a sensation lasting into the 1980s. It was in the Venetian Room that Tony Bennett first performed "I Left my Heart in San Francisco." Guests enjoyed performances by other musical legends such as Ella Fitzgerald, B. B. King, The Roches, and Marlene Dietrich. (The Fairmont Hotel.)

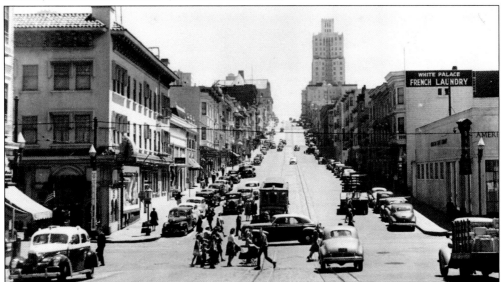

On the eastern slope of Nob Hill following World War II, California and Polk Streets are bustling with cable cars, a baby buggy, a delivery truck, and the French laundry. The unfinished Grace Cathedral building is visible at the crest of the hill on the left, unobscured by the high-rise apartment building that would be built on the near corner of Jones Street.

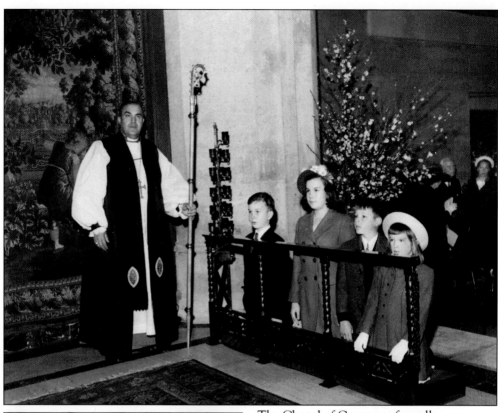

The Chapel of Grace was formally dedicated on the March 16, 1948.

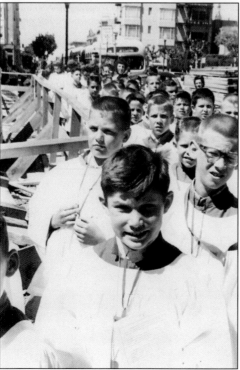

Even as construction continued, processions made their way along the Taylor Street edge of the former Crocker family property.

Life at Grace Cathedral continued in praise and celebration, as exhibited by these choristers. Michael Lampen is in the center of the first row. A son of Canon Lampen and Betty Grubb Lampen, Michael was to become the cathedral archivist. The other boys are unidentified.

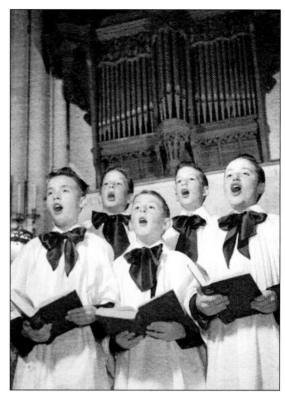

Choristers appear in a more candid photograph a few years later.

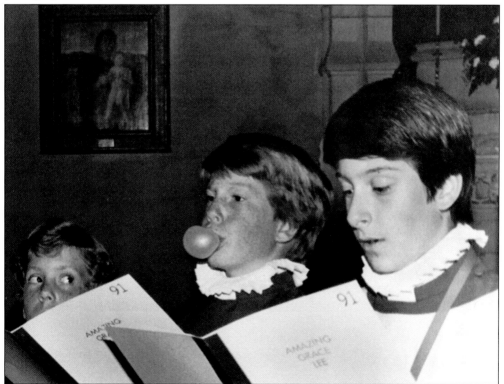

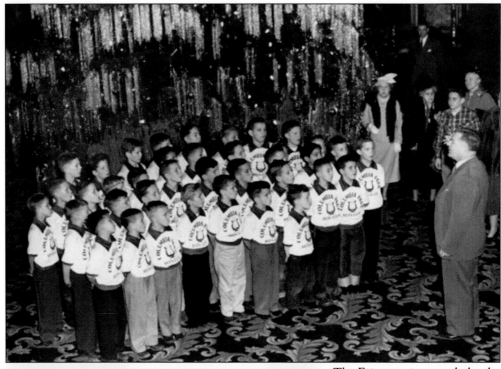

The Fairmont is a wonderland of surprise during the winter holidays. On December 22, 1950, William B. Maltby directs a group from the Columbia Park Boys Club in a rehearsal of Christmas carols in the lobby.

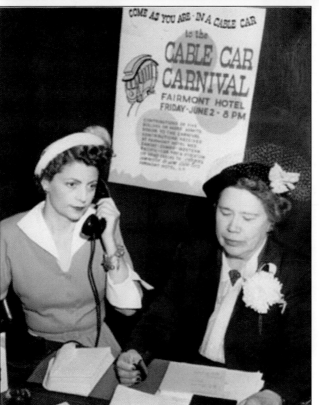

Neighborhood events on Nob Hill have included festive competitions among hotel staff, with waiters racing up California Street bearing trays of drinks, Easter parades, and a Cable Car Carnival at the Fairmont Hotel. Vera Schwabacher (left) and Mrs. Norman Smith help to see that the carnival progresses smoothly.

This fashion show in the Peacock Room of the Mark Hopkins Hotel is well attended.

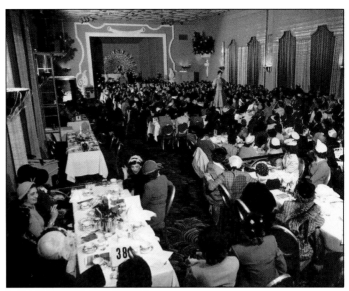

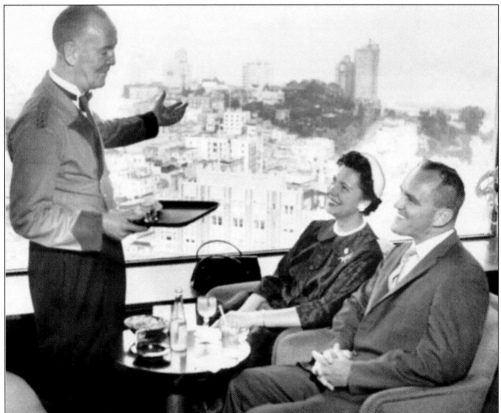

The Top of the Mark, where military men had bid farewell to their wives and sweethearts before heading out to battle in the Pacific, attracted veterans and anyone seeking to recapture the romance of the war years—without the cloud of war obscuring the view. Today the bandstand still sees talented combos playing music to inspire dancing couples, and the view of San Francisco and the vast Pacific still provide a breathtaking vista from the Top of the Mark.

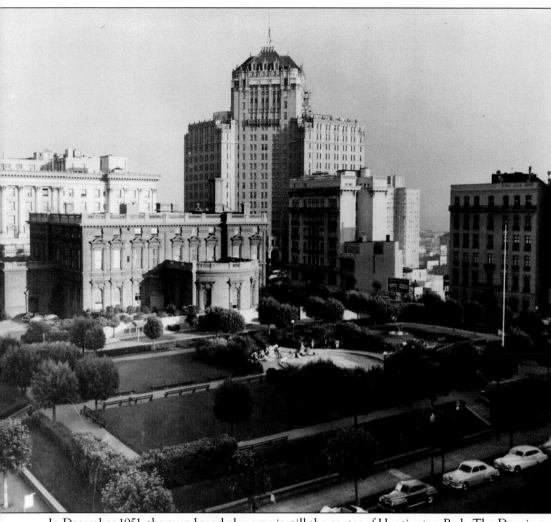

In December 1951, the round sand play area is still the center of Huntington Park. The Dancing Sprites (southeast lawn area) frolick in the sun as they do today.

In 1955, Huntington Park received La Fontana delle Tartarughe (The Tortoise Fountain), a gift from the family of Mrs. William Crocker. On the story of the fountain's journey to the United States, historian Phillip Elissetche cites two sources: one stating that Crocker purchased the fountain from a villa near Rome that was being subdivided in 1924 and the other that William H. Crocker bought the fountain in 1906 and had it brought to the garden of the Crocker's New Place estate, in Hillsborough, in 1911. The fountain is seen here in Hillsborough. (Phil Elissetche.)

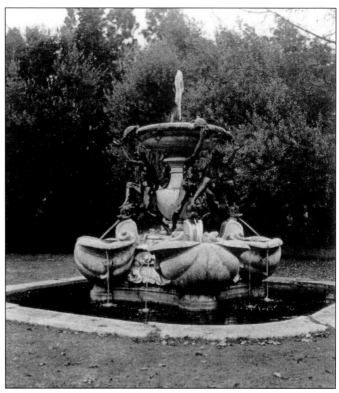

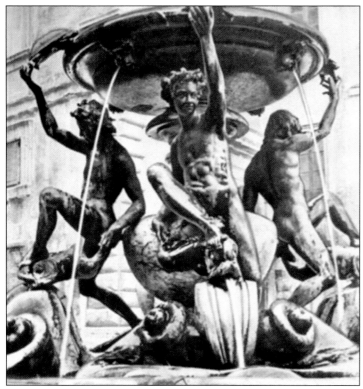

According to Phillip Elissetche's research, the original Fontana delle Tartarughe was completed in 1588 and is situated in the Piazza Mattei in Rome. Copies were made by the Chiurazzi foundry, in Naples, from 1900 to 1930. Ethel Crocker, who died in 1952, bequeathed her copy to the San Francisco Recreation and Park Department. In 1955, the fountain was brought from the Crocker estate in Hillsborough to Huntington Park. (Phil Elissetche.)

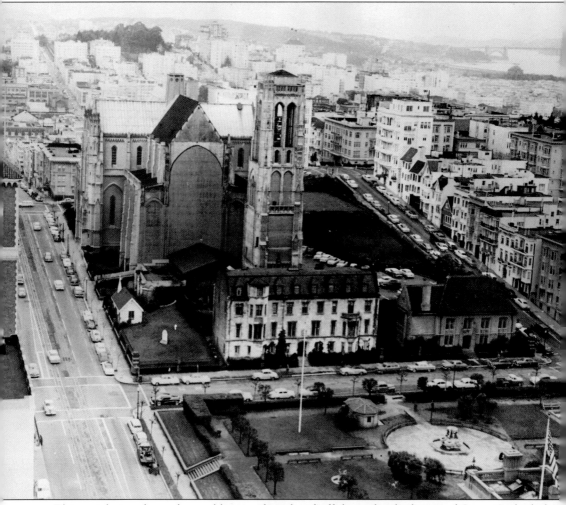

This aerial view shows the steel barrier that closed off the unfinished nave of Grace Cathedral until the building was completed in the early 1960s, and the base awaits the fleche. The Wayside Chapel sits on the southern edge of the property. In Huntington Park, the Fountain of the Sprites and Fontana delle Tartarughe are both in place. In the distance, Fort Point keeps watch over the Golden Gate, and the south tower of the Golden Gate Bridge is visible. The bridge was begun and finished in a fraction of the time that it took to realize the dream of the great cathedral building.

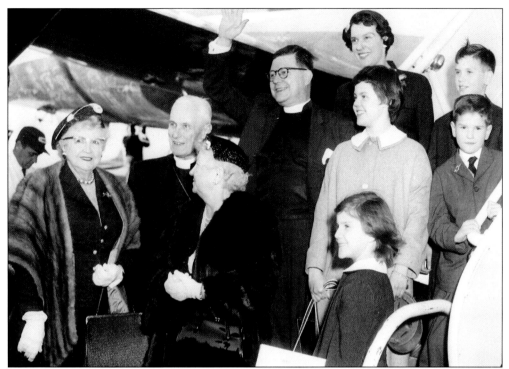

In 1958, James Pike succeeded Karl Morgan Block as bishop of California. This photograph was taken upon the arrival of Bishop Pike (the younger man in a clerical collar) and his family. The bishop's controversial politics and personal life would prove a great challenge to the diocese.

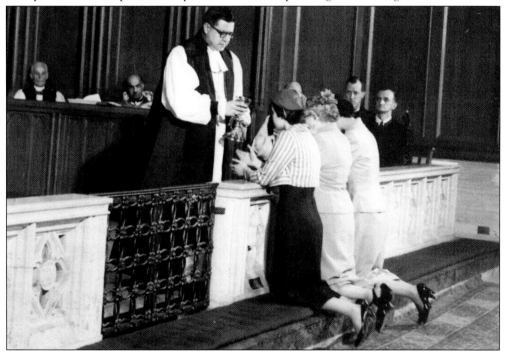

Bishop Pike distributes the Eucharist to his mother, wife, and daughter.

PROCLAMATION

GROUND BREAKING CEREMONY   CALIFORNIA MASONIC MEMORIAL TEMPLE

One of the most important of the matters which have engaged my attention has been the plans for building the new California Masonic Memorial Temple. The need is obvious. When I was Grand Orator in 1941—with a membership of about 126,000 and some 582 Lodges—even then the facilities on Van Ness Avenue were far too cramped. Now that we have grown with our great State to 225,000 members and 655 Lodges, the need is just that much more acute.

The Temple thus will be adequate housing for year round administrative activities and for our annual events. It will be a memorial also to those Brethren of our armed forces who gave their lives that we might live, a beacon to light the way to Masonry for us and our children, and a symbol high in the western sky to inspire all true lovers of American freedom.

It also will be a place where you, your friends and families may visit and linger while enjoying a "billion dollar view."

I am pleased, therefore, that the Most Worshipful Edward H. Siems, Chairman of the Memorial Building Committee, and the Most Worshipful Lloyd E. Wilson, Grand Secretary, report to me the following progress: We own, free and clear, the site atop Nob Hill, for which we paid $730,000.00. This land and the money on hand from contributions and some other sources is about $1,900,000.00. Of this, the campaign to date has produced $1,145,000.00 from 67,613 contributors. The campaign will continue and at the present rate of receipts it is expected as of October this year to produce an additional $75,000.00.

Funds of $2,750,000.00 and an additional $250,000.00, if required, have been offered by six banks. The loan would bear 4% interest on money if and as used, on a ten-year period, and with the privilege of accelerating payments. This loan could be retired from the present $1.00 per capita, producing about $225,000.00 a year, and the present $9.00 per Candidate, producing about $75,000.00 a year, both items having been written into our Ordinances. This would make a total of $300,000.00 available annually. Also, there would be available from the completed structure income of the garage designed for 450 cars and rentals of the auditorium. Surveys have estimated this combined income at $100,000.00 a year.

Consequently, I have decided that as of October this year the time will have been reached to START CONSTRUCTION. Having in mind that we shall meet in Annual Communication commencing October 24, I therefore proclaim *Wednesday, October 26, "Ground Breaking Day,"* to be observed by the Craft in Grand Lodge assembled. Features of the Day will include a public Ceremony at the Site commemorating the event and bearing witness to "the untiring, unending industry of the Free and Accepted Masons of California and Hawaii."

All honor to the 67,613 members whose contributions have made possible the program thus far! Their participation is sincerely appreciated.

Your help by continued support and by contributions is necessary. Send your contribution through your Lodge Secretary so your Lodge may meet its quota. This will also enable you to say "*I was part of the building of the Temple and of this new epoch in the history of California Masonry.*"

Attest:

Lloyd E. Wilson   *Henry C. Clausen*
GRAND MASTER

It was in 1947 that the Grand Lodge of California Freemasons recommended that a new temple be built to meet its needs and requirements. Property at 1111 California Street, the former site of the Towne house, famous for its portal, was purchased and a modern building was designed. (Grand Lodge of California Freemasons.)

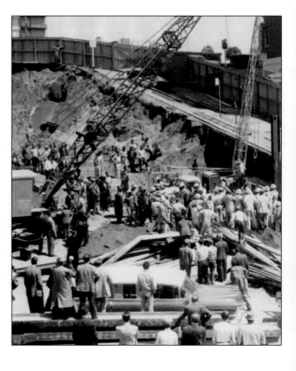

During construction of the Masonic Temple, a workman fell into a wall cavity. A fellow worker attempted to rescue him, but to no avail. The second man made it to safety, but the first man was crushed to death. (Grand Lodge of California Freemasons.)

The enormous mosaic window depicts those who came to California and founded Freemasonry in the state. California artist Emile Norman, known as an iconoclast, used the endomosaic process, incorporating stained glass and small pieces of metal, textiles, paper, natural foliage, and the remains of seashells and sea life. All of California's 58 counties and the Hawaiian Islands are represented in soil included in the lower portion of the window. Norman was assisted in this and much of his work by his life partner, Brooks Clement. (Grand Lodge of California Freemasons.)

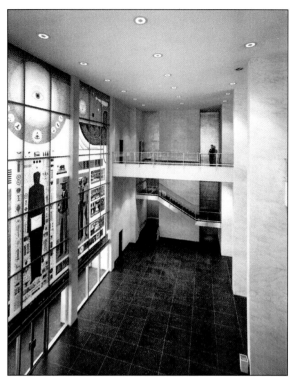

The Masonic Temple was dedicated on September 29, 1958, with much attendant pomp, ritual, and excitement. (Grand Lodge of California Freemasons.)

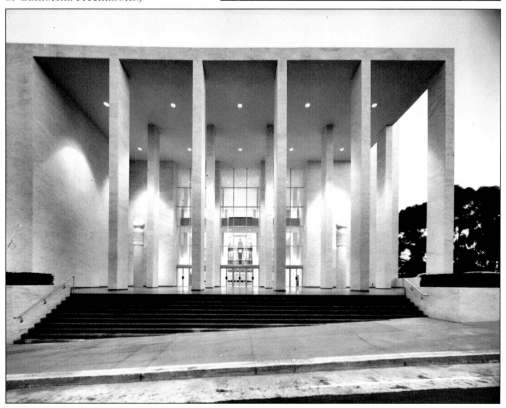

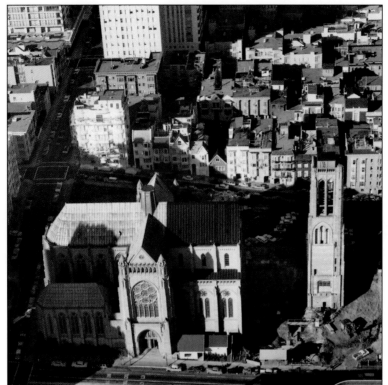

As the 1950s
became the 1960s,
Grace Cathedral
was yet unfinished.

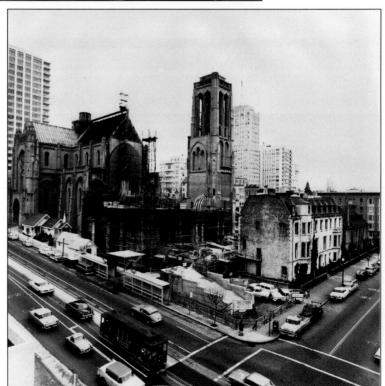

The bell tower,
dedicated in 1943,
seems to patiently
wait for the
cathedral building
to be done and
the fleche to stand
atop its base.

The Wayside Chapel, nestled beside the south wall, provided a 24-hour house of worship for all.

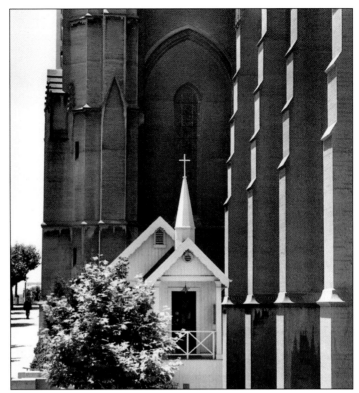

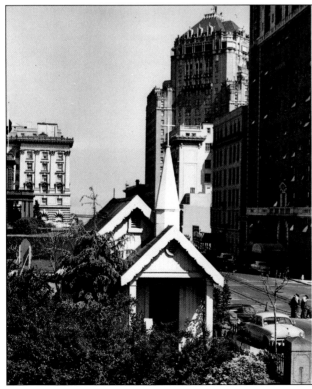

Had this photograph been taken prior to April 1906, the Wayside Chapel would have been on the Crocker family's property. On the site of the Huntington Hotel (near right) was the Tobin residence. Where the Mark Hopkins Hotel is (in the background at right) stood the spectacular Hopkins mansion. The Fairmont Hotel (left) would have been under construction. The front of the Pacific-Union Club building, then the Flood residence, appeared much the same. The Coulton-Huntington residence stood in the place of Huntington Park.

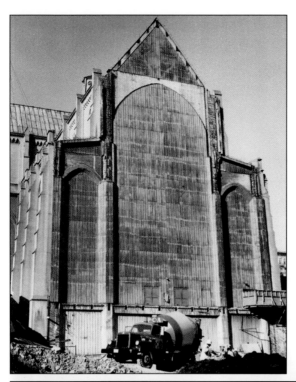

This photograph by Portland Cement Association provides a striking look at the great steel wall that marked the place where the progress of the cathedral building was suspended.

The roof of the Mark Hopkins is elaborately decorated in lights on New Year's Eve, 1962. (San Francisco Public Library.)

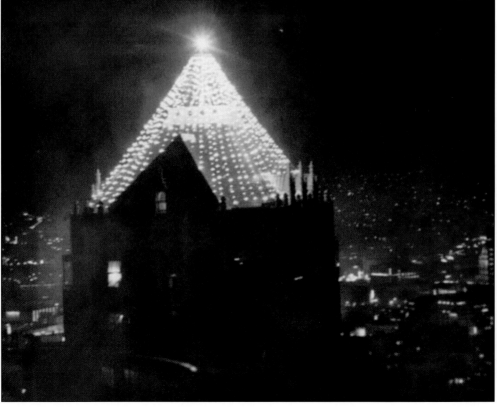

In 1963, modernity is being
exhibited at the Fairmont. (San
Francisco Public Library.)

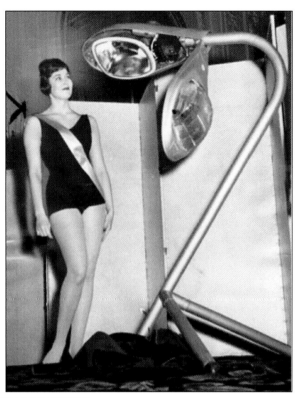

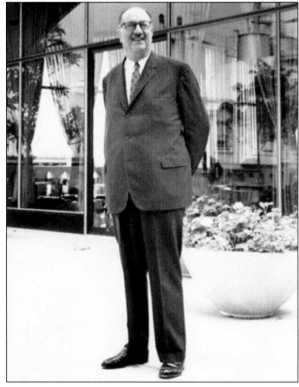

Benjamin Swig enjoys his domain
in the roof garden at the Fairmont.
(San Francisco Public Library.)

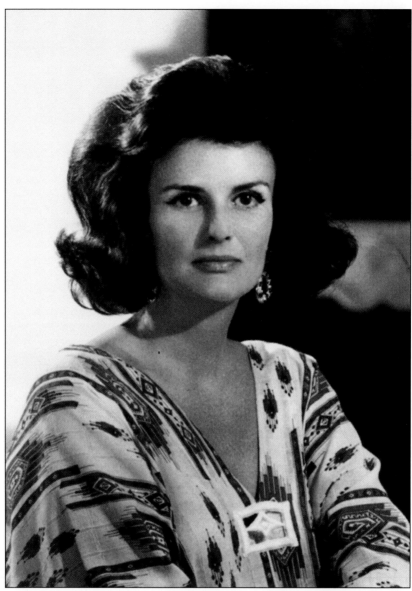

The Hungtington Apartments became the Huntington Hotel Apartments in 1942 when Eugene Fritz acquired the building. The apartments were converted into guest rooms, resulting in unusually spacious hotel accommodations. With Eugene Fritz at the helm, the hotel developed a reputation for luxury and sophistication. In the previous century, Fritz's ancestor Mary Fritz had accomplished the daunting task of creating Ashbury Heights from the steep hills to the west of Buena Vista Park. The diminutive Mary Fritz had been scoffed at in the male-dominated world of real estate development, but Ashbury Heights remains a stunning and vibrant neighborhood and is home to the current mayor, Gavin Newsome. When still a teenager, Dorothy Fritz, better known as "Dolly," became owner of the Huntington, and the hotel continued its fine tradition. Dorothy "Dolly" Fritz (pictured here) was outgoing and adventuresome, with a memorable style and spirit. She and husband Newton Cope kept the Huntington a quietly sophisticated hotel. Isabelle and Serena Fritz Cope, daughters of Dorothy, maintained the understated elegance. The Huntington continues to draw guests with its elegance and charm. (Ron Henggeler.)

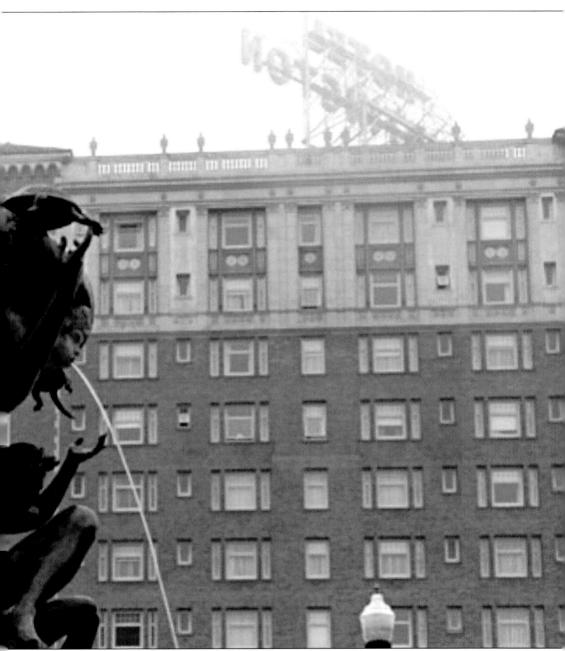

Dorothy "Dolly" Fritz's can be compared to the fictional "Eloise," who lives at the Plaza Hotel, but with a rather significant difference: Dolly owned her hotel. Dolly Fritz's daughters became second-generation "Eloises" and have memories of glimpsing grand parties at the hotel, before being taken across Huntington Square to their home and their beds.

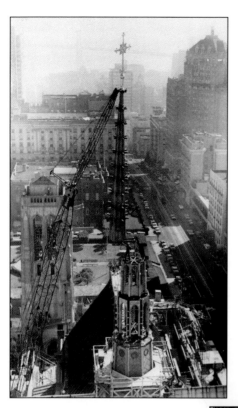

At last, the cathedral building was completed, the flèche was hoisted into place, and the Grace Episcopal Cathedral was dedicated in 1964!

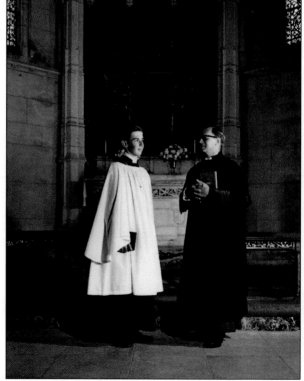

Canon Lampen and his son Michael, in his choir vestments, share a moment in the Chapel of Grace, where Michael's parents were married in 1945.

A young Billy Graham is escorted at Grace Cathedral by Bishop Pike. The charismatic bishop was deeply committed to political activism. He was active in the civil rights movement and ordained a woman to the diaconate despite official objections. He also advocated the acceptance of LGBT people by churches. Pike was a proponent of reproductive rights and the rights of workers to make a living wage. He abdicated in 1966. In 1969, James Pike died after his car broke down in the Israeli desert. He is buried at the Protestant cemetery at Jaffa.

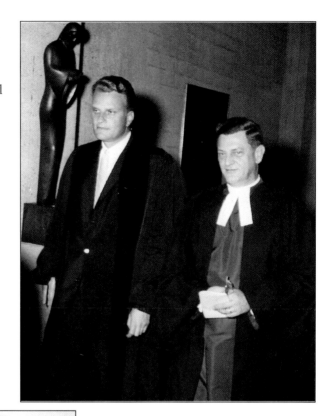

GRÁCE
CÁTHEDRÁL
PRESENTS
A
CONCERT
OF
SÁCRED MUSIC
BY
DUKE
ELLINGTON

Thursday, September 16, 1965
San Francisco, California

In celebration of the dedication of the cathedral, Duke Ellington and his orchestra performed on September 16, 1965.

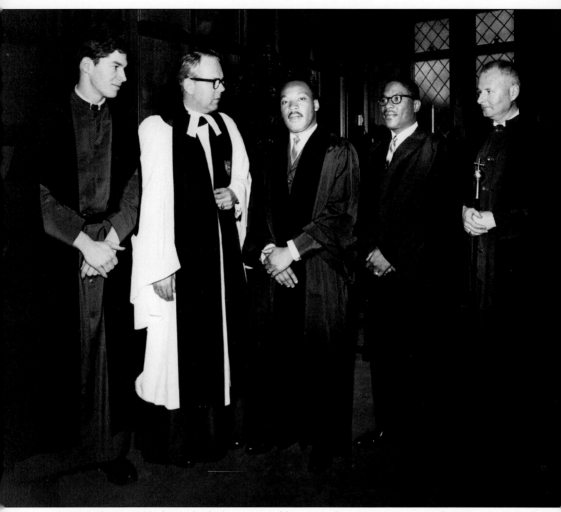

On March 28, 1965, the cathedral was graced by a visit from Rev. Martin Luther King Jr. From left to right are Assistant Verger John Seaman, Vice Dean Robert Haggard, Dr. King, his unidentified aide, and longtime Verger Charles Agneau.

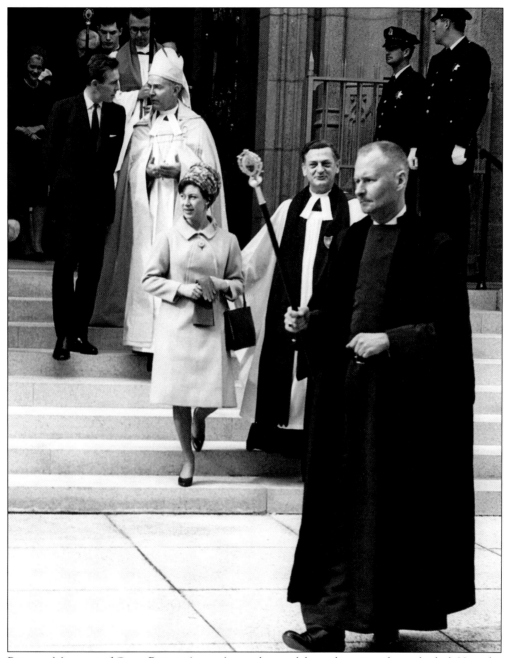

Princess Margaret of Great Britain (center) was also a celebrated guest at the cathedral. Here she is seen being escorted by the Very Reverend C. Julian Bartlett. Lord Snowdon is at left, behind the princess.

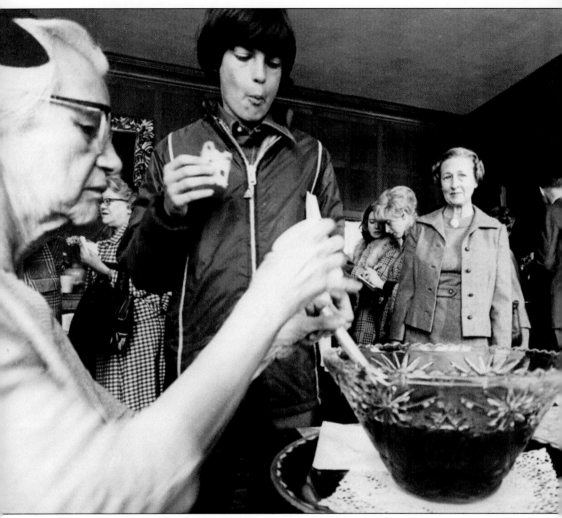

Times change, but the tradition of coffee hour endures. Here it is encapsulated, with Ernestine Gardiner at the punch ladle.

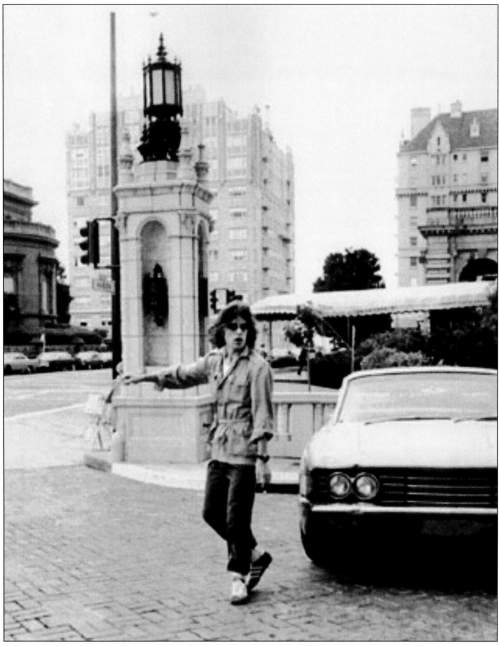

Down the street from Grace Cathedral, Mick Jagger does not hide from the paparazzi during his stay at the Mark Hopkins. (Mark Hopkins Intercontinental Hotel.)

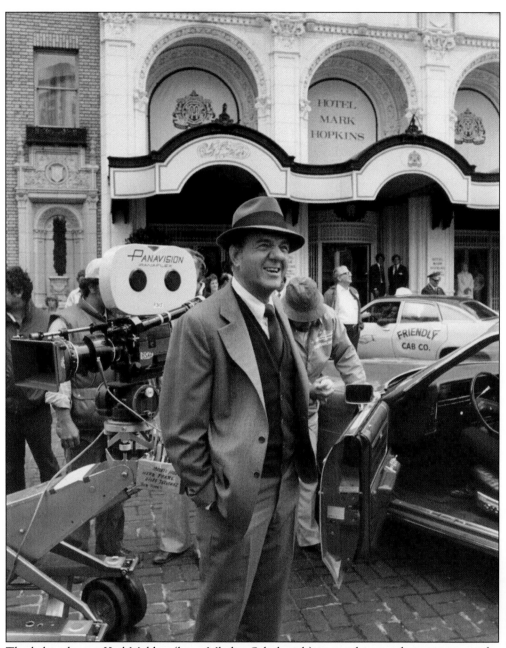

The beloved actor Karl Malden (born Mladen Sekulovich) is seen here at the entrance to the Mark Hopkins Hotel during filming for the television crime series *The Streets of San Francisco*, which ran from September 1972 through the 1977 season. Malden portrayed Mike Stone, a widowed homicide detective, with 20 years on the police force of his native city. The popular series, filmed on location, brought scenes of San Francisco into millions of homes. (Mark Hopkins Intercontinental Hotel.)

Six

TRANSFORMATION

The windswept crest that became the centerpiece of Nob Hill has had many faces. A weather-beaten hill, a collection of pioneer houses, the site of sumptuous residences—"Clay Street Hill," "California Street Hill," finally "Nob Hill" changed rapidly from the 1840s to the 20th century.

For a short while, after the great disaster in 1906, Nob Hill, like the rest of the city east of Van Ness Avenue, was the scene of devastation. Then, with the rest of San Francisco, Nob Hill emerged renewed in unanticipated ways. There are grand hotels, luxury apartments, artists ateliers, and musicians' digs. The huge Masonic Temple is across the intersection from the intimate neighborhood park. An exclusive club sits opposite a "house of prayer for all people." The 1970s brought challenges for the Nob Hill neighborhood. A recession and a changed society meant that people's attention was focused on difficult issues. In 1978, a height limit was set on construction on Nob Hill, addressing the problem of obliterated views and loss of sunlight. In the early 1980s, the Nob Hill Association executed a successful campaign to restore Huntington Park.

The Very Reverend Alan Jones was dean of Grace Cathedral from 1985 until his retirement on January 31, 2009. His theology is progressive and his sermons invite congregants to accept the challenge of forgiveness. During the 1990s, major changes were made to the cathedral buildings, resulting in the creation of a plaza and fountain in the close, a new diocesan house, subterranean parking facilities, and a renovated crypt. Early in the 21st century, Huntington Park curator Phillip Elissetche oversaw the restoration of La Fontana delle Tartarughe.

Amid mostly polite conflicts between public and private, progressive and conservative, canine and human, and the like, Nob Hill is in its second century as a center of San Francisco's social, religious, creative, and civic lives. Sightings of ghosts of troubled souls from earlier times are reported, and many ghosts are kept private. One may walk along California Street admiring the modernity of the Masonic Temple and the next minute find oneself on Taylor Street gazing at the stone fence of the Crocker residence, where charring from the 1906 fire is still visible. Nob Hill is rich with both the history of San Francisco and the everyday comings and goings of San Franciscans and visitors alike.

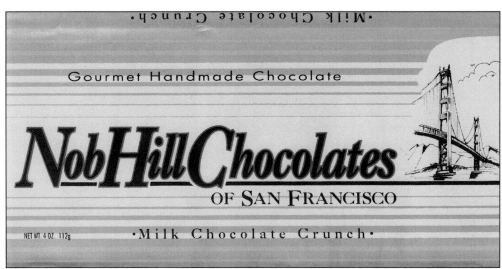

A confectioner produced Nob Hill chocolates for a time. Would they have been stocked in the larders of the great residences that once stood on this fabled hill?

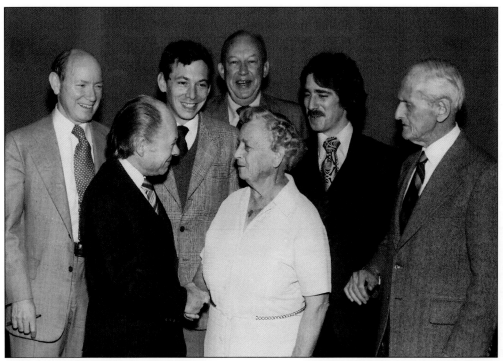

This gathering on the occasion of one of many concerts by visiting organists are Paul Callaway, organist Washington National Cathedral (shaking the hand of the organist, who is not identified); Eric Hubert, cathedral trustee (far left); John Fenstermaker, Grace cathedral organist (wearing a sweater); Paul Pearson, Cathedral School teacher (back), and two unidentified men on the right.

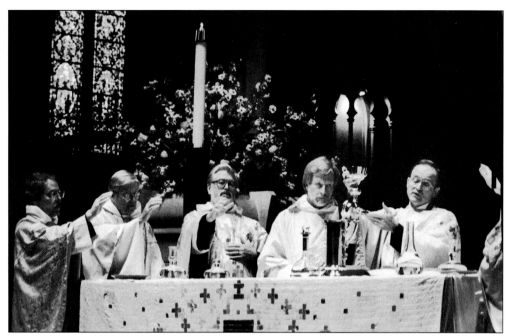

At the Grace Cathedral altar, the Right Reverend William Swing (right), who became the seventh bishop of the Diocese of California in 1979, celebrates the Eucharist with the Very Reverend Alan Jones (center), dean of the cathedral from 1985 until January 2009.

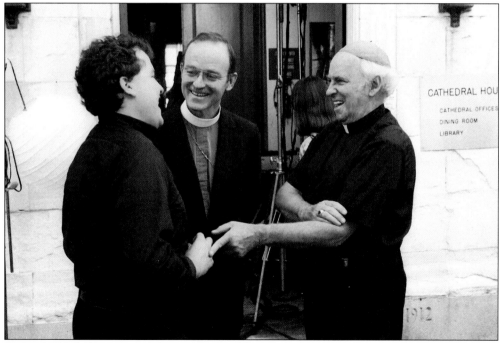

Grace Cathedral has appeared in cameos and featured roles in many television shows and films, including Alfred Hitcock's final film, *Family Plot*. During the filming of the 1985 movie *Maxie*, which also starred Glenn Close and Ruth Gordon, director Paul Aaron (left) and actor Barnard Hughes (right) enjoy a laugh with Bishop William Swing.

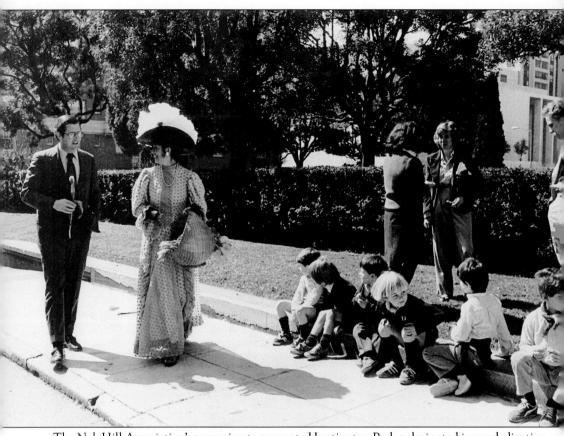

The Nob Hill Association's campaign to renovate Huntington Park culminated in a rededication in the early 1980s. Some of those attending wore 19th-century dress. (Nob Hill Association.)

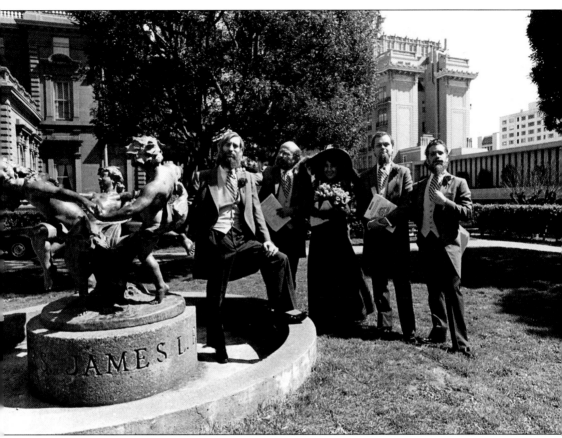

Members of the USF Players (University of San Francisco) played the roles of some of the Associates and their wives. The university thespians were honored to participate and had a marvelous time, according to a letter they sent to the Nob Hill Association after the event. (Nob Hill Association.)

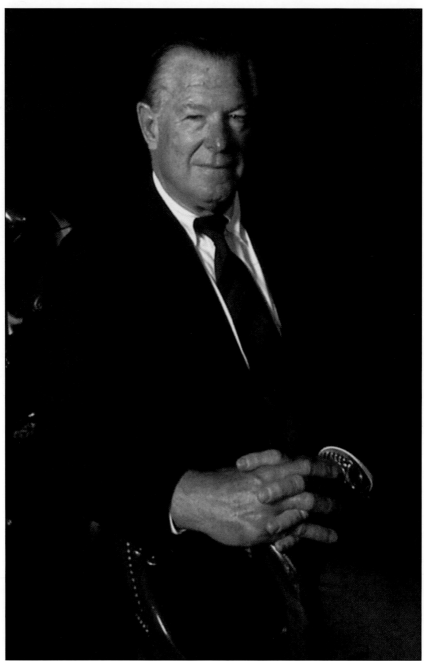

Newton Cope of Sacramento became a real estate investor in 1959. In 1967, Cope married Dorothy "Dolly" Fritz MacMasters, who had owned the Huntington Hotel since she was a teenager. Cope adopted Dolly's two daughters, Marguerite and Isabelle, and he and Dolly had two other children, Serena and Callaghan, together. Cope became president of Nob Hill Properties, Incorporated, in 1976, since which time the real estate company has acquired many additional properties. In 1979, the marriage of Newton Cope and Lee Radziwill was called off just a few minutes before the ceremony was to begin. Apparently, the bride's sister, Jacqueline Kennedy Onassis, nixed the union. Cope died in November 2005, after suffering from cancer. (Ron Henggeler.)

Dean Alan Jones and Mayor Frank Jordan appeared at the ground-breaking for the new cathedral close and chapter house.

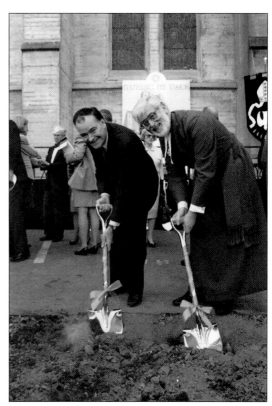

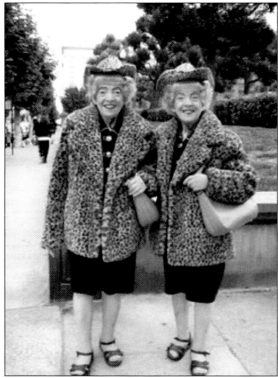

Identical twins Marian and Vivian Brown were born January 25th, 1927, in Kalamazoo, Michigan. They moved to San Francisco in 1970 and worked as secretaries in downtown offices. They are fixtures of Nob Hill, delighting locals and visitors alike with their eye-catching identical outfits. (Karen Morgan, www.blackbird-bakery.com)

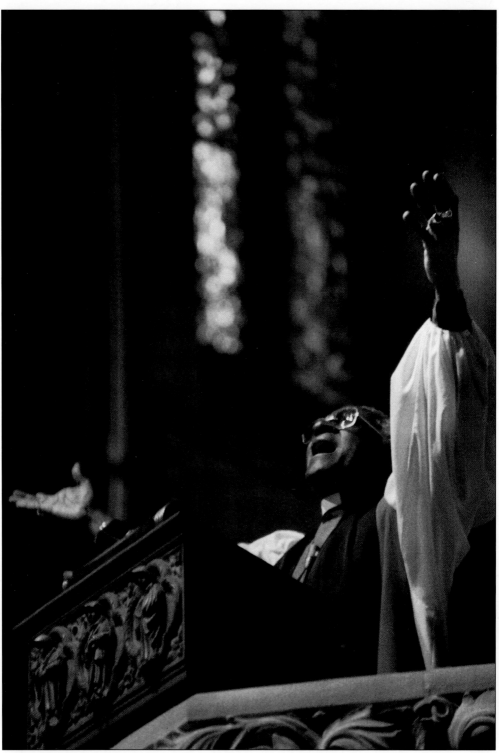

Archbishop Desmond Tutu has visited Grace Cathedral on more than one occasion, bringing messages of hope and reconciliation.

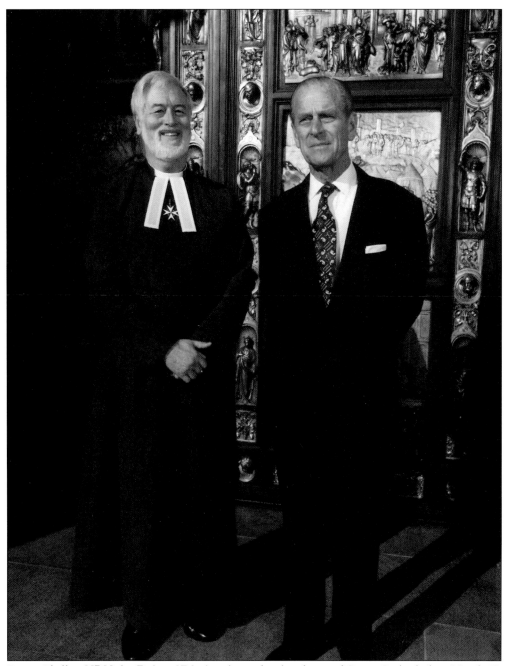

Prince Phillip, HRH the Duke of Edinburgh, made a brief tour of Grace Cathedral on March 17, 1998, accompanied by the Very Reverend Alan Jones, dean of the cathedral.

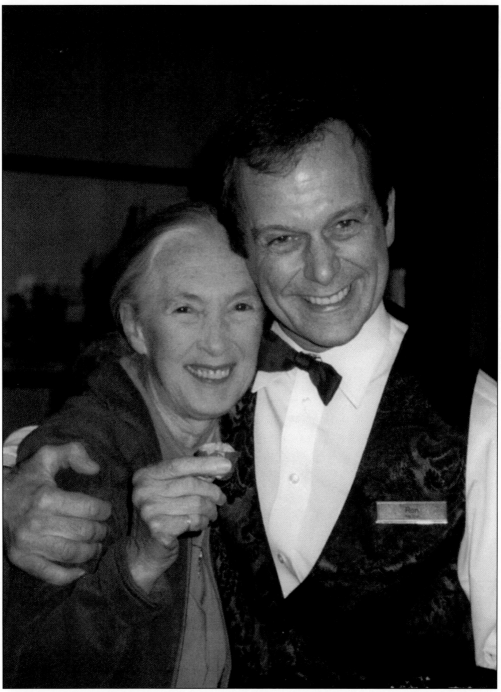

Dame Jane Goodall, the British primatologist and UN messenger of peace, is a favorite visitor to Nob Hill. A friend of Alan Jones, she has been a guest on *The Forum at Grace Cathedral*, a series of conversations with prominent figures held since 1995. Goodall has also made friends among the staff at the Huntington, who speak fondly of her warmth and good humor. (Ron Henggeler.)

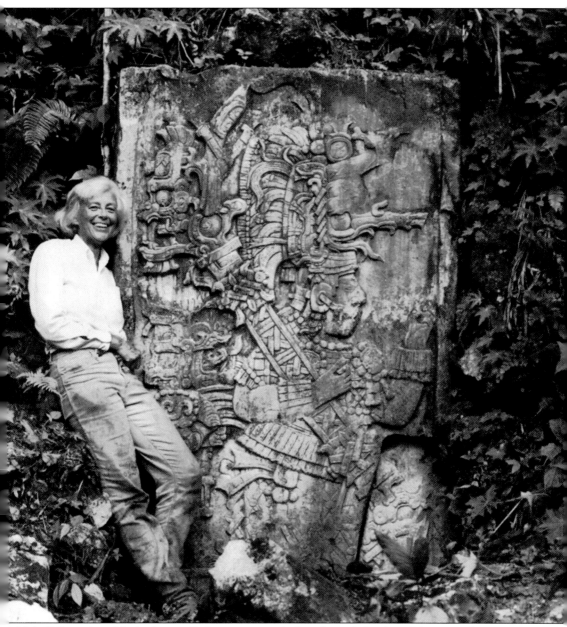

Nob Hill resident Merle Greene Robertson is a scholar of pre-Columbian Mayan civilization. An artist, she developed a technique of doing rubbings of Mayan monuments, of which she has done thousands. Through her work as an archaeologist and art historian, she has done much to preserve Mayan cultural artifacts and history. (Ron Henggeler.)

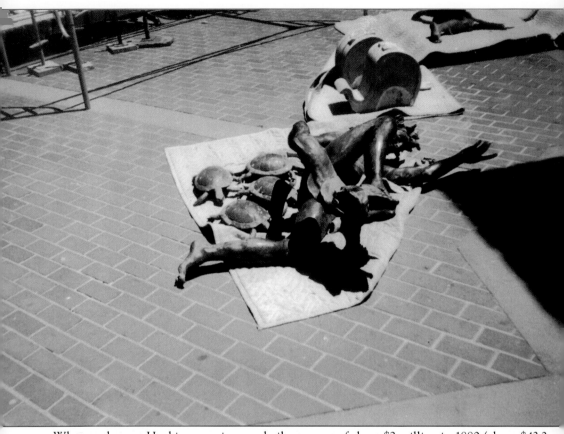

Whereas the vast Hopkins mansion was built at a cost of about $2 million in 1880 (about $43.2 million in 2010 dollars), it took a $500,000 fund-raising campaign to restore the Fountain of the Tortoises in 2001.

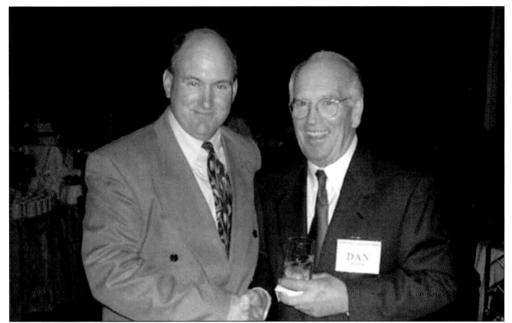

Phil Elissetche (left), Huntington Park groundskeeper, received accolades from the Nob Hill Association and the City of San Francisco for his painstaking research and hands-on involvement in the restoration of the fountain. (Phil Elissetche.)

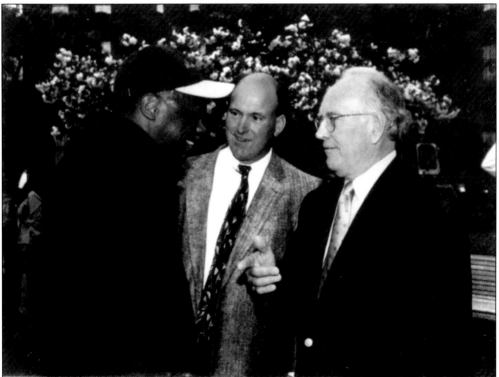

Mayor Willie Brown (left), Phil Elissetche (center), and Stephen Patton celebrate the rededication of La Fontana delle Tartarughe. (Phil Elissetche.)

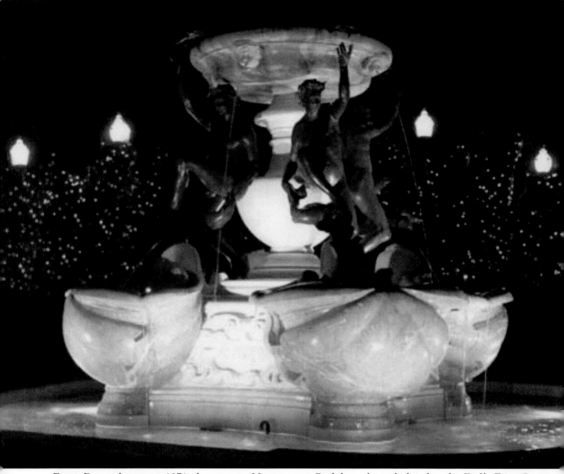

Every December since 1971, the trees in Huntington Park have been lighted at the Dolly Fritz-Cope Tree Lighting. The Nob Hill Association directs the festivities. Neighbors and dignitaries gather, and members of the San Francisco Girls' Chorus perform seasonal songs. (Phil Elissetche.)

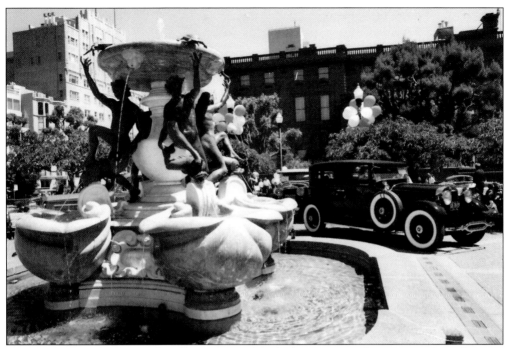

Each year, the California Mille offers guests a close look at sports and racing cars from the years 1927 through 1957. The event in Huntington Park is a benefit for the Nob Hill Association. (Nob Hill Association.)

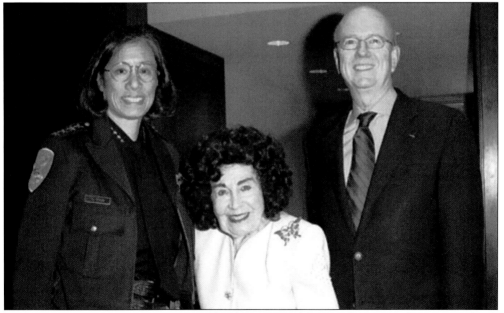

Isabella "Bella" Farrow was born in Oakland in 1922 and became known as the Queen of Nob Hill. A tireless fund-raiser, she collected over $2 million for St. Francis Hospital with an annual black-tie benefit, Hob Nob on the Hill. In 2004, she hosted six major fund-raising events. In this 2004 photograph, she is flanked by Chief of Police Heather Fong and Tom Horn, of the Nob Hill Association's board of directors. Farrow died in 2010.. (Photograph by Caesar Alexzander.)

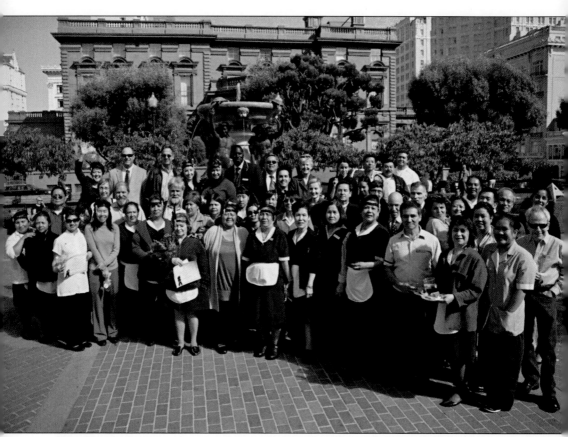

Ron Henggeler's photograph shows Huntington Hotel owners and staff. Behind the group, La Fontana delle Tartarughe bubbles in the sunlight. The balustrade on the former Flood residence crowns the Connecticut sandstone, as always. Fabled buildings sit discreetly along the south side of California Street. If the walls at the Mark Hopkins Hotel could talk, they might relate what First Lady Michelle Obama, First Daughters Sasha and Malia, and Marian Robinson, Michelle's mother, talked about before turning in during their stay in June 2009. Behind the Flood residence, the Fairmont Hotel stands, always ready to welcome guests with elegance and efficiency, thanks in great part to Tom Wolfe, America's first concierge. The Brocklebank (far left) seems to keep watch over children in the park, men coming and going at the Pacific-Union Club, socialites, scoundrels, clergy, hospitality experts, heads of state, tourists, pilgrims, neighboring Chinatown, North Beach, and Russian Hill, and mysteries that many will never know.

INDEX

DISCOVER THOUSANDS OF LOCAL HISTORY BOOKS FEATURING MILLIONS OF VINTAGE IMAGES

Arcadia Publishing, the leading local history publisher in the United States, is committed to making history accessible and meaningful through publishing books that celebrate and preserve the heritage of America's people and places.

Find more books like this at
www.arcadiapublishing.com

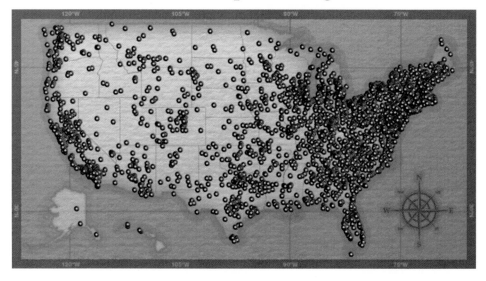

Search for your hometown history, your old stomping grounds, and even your favorite sports team.

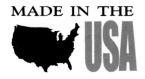